Contents

P9-DEY-385

Introduction

Japan is a beguiling mix of opposites – old and new, east and west; the most modern of countries, it retains at the same time its ancient traditions and an awareness of thousands of years of history. This is the country of crazy modern buildings and ancient castles; of energy, wealth and of serene Buddhist temples. It is a nation like nowhere else on earth.

Japan is a giant of business, technology, food, fashion, architecture, animation and art. Trends shift at a breathtaking pace, but this is also a country that was closed to the world until around 140 years ago, and it mixes its modernity with huge doses of ancient tradition. You might find Western fast-food outlets beside a millennium-old temple, or a cacophony of screaming LCD screens just a few paces from a historic eatery. It's this beguiling mishmash of old and new that makes Japan so exciting to explore.

Travelling the country is a joy. It's safe, welcoming and staggeringly efficient. Japan's reputation for outrageous prices is well founded, but it also has plenty on offer for the budget traveller. You can eat well here on a shoestring budget, and the budget hotel sector is booming. Of course, if you have the cash to splash, there is no shortage of luxury, from sumptuous hotels to sushi restaurants. Either way, the sights, sounds and flavours are priceless.

Most visits begin in Tokyo, the world's largest metropolis, where towering architecture, blinking neon and outrageous fashions will mesmerise you, but to get a true taste of this unique destination you also need to take in the temple-laden streets of historic Kyoto, the volcanic terrain of Kyushu, the majestic Mount Fuji, the indigenous culture of Hokkaido and the serenity of a hot-spring resort.

THOMAS COOK'S JAPAN

On 11 May 1874, Cook's *Excursionist and Tourist Advertiser* contained the words: 'We … have in contemplation the establishment of an agency in Japan.' By 1904 there was an annual spring tour by steamer and Pullman to 'the land of cherry blossom' and in 1906 the first office opened in Yokohama. The coronation of Emperor Taisho in 1915 inspired great interest. Cook's developed tours to the most remote parts of the country, reminding its travellers that for all its quaintness, Japan even in the 1920s was a fully Westernised country: 'Even the humble cottage of the farmer in a remote village is lighted by electricity.'

As one of the world's longest established
and best-known travel brands,
Thomas Cook are the experts in travel.

For more than 135 years our
guidebooks have unlocked the secrets
of destinations around the world,
sharing with travellers a wealth of
experience and a passion for travel.

**Rely on Thomas Cook as your
travelling companion on your next trip
and benefit from our unique heritage.**

Thomas Cook **traveller** guides

JAPAN
Lesley Chan

Thomas
Cook

Your travelling companion since 1873

Written by Lesley Chan, updated by Nick Coldicott
Original photography by Jim Holmes, James Montgomery and Will Robb

Published by Thomas Cook Publishing
A division of Thomas Cook Tour Operations Limited.
Company Registration no. 3772199 England
The Thomas Cook Business Park, Unit 9, Coningsby Road,
Peterborough PE3 8SB, United Kingdom
Email: books@thomascook.com, Tel: + 44 (0) 1733 416477
www.thomascookpublishing.com

Produced by Cambridge Publishing Management Limited
Burr Elm Court, Main Street, Caldecote CB23 7NU

ISBN: 978-1-84848-241-8

© 2004, 2006, 2008 Thomas Cook Publishing
This fourth edition © 2010
Text © Thomas Cook Publishing,
Maps © Thomas Cook Publishing/PCGraphics (UK) Limited
Transport map © Communicarta Limited

Series Editor: Linda Bass
Production/DTP: Steven Collins

Cover photography © Thomas Cook

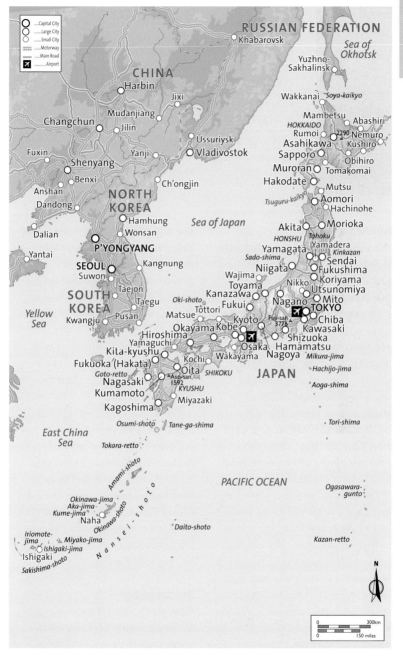

- ○ — Capital City
- ○ — Large City
- ○ — Small City
- ═══ — Motorway
- ▬▬ — Main Road
- ✈ — Airport

RUSSIAN FEDERATION

Khabarovsk

Sea of Okhotsk

Yuzhno-Sakhalinsk

CHINA

Harbin

Jixi

Wakkanai   *Soya-kaikyo*

Mambetsu

HOKKAIDO   Abashiri

Changchun   Mudanjiang   Jilin

Rumoi   2290   Nemuro

Asahikawa   Kushiro

Fuxin   Yanji   Ussuriysk

Sapporo   Obihiro

Shenyang   Vladivostok

Muroran   Tomakomai

Benxi   Ch'ongjin

Hakodate   Mutsu

Anshan

Tsuguru-kaikyo   Aomori

Dandong

NORTH KOREA

Hachinohe

Dalian   Hamhung   *Sea of Japan*

Akita   Morioka

Wonsan

HONSHU   *Tohoku*

Yantai   **P'YONGYANG**

Yamagata   *Yamadera*

Sado-shima   *Kinkazan*

SEOUL   Kangnung

Niigata   Sendai

Suwon

Fukushima

SOUTH KOREA   Taejon   Wajima   Nikko   Koriyama

Toyama   Utsunomiya

Kanazawa   Nagano   Mito

Yellow Sea   Taegu   *Oki-shoto*   Fukui   ✈TOKYO

Kwangju   Pusan   Matsue   *Tottori*   Kyoto   Chiba

Fuji-san

Okayama Kobe   3776   Kawasaki

Hiroshima   ✈Osaka   Shizuoka

Yamaguchi   Hamamatsu

Kita-kyushu   Kochi   Wakayama   Nagoya   *Mikura-jima*

Fukuoka (Hakata)   Oita   *SHIKOKU*   **JAPAN**   *Hachijo-jima*

Goto-retto   *Aso-san*

Nagasaki   1592   *Aoga-shima*

KYUSHU

Kumamoto   Miyazaki

Kagoshima

Osumi-shoto   *Tane-ga-shima*   *Tori-shima*

East China Sea   *Tokara-retto*

Ogasawara-gunto

Amami-shoto

PACIFIC OCEAN

Okinawa-jima
Aka-jima
Kume-jima   Naha

Okinawa-shoto

Iriomote-jima   Miyako-jima   *Daito-shoto*   *Kazan-retto*

Ishigaki-jima

Ishigaki

Sakishima-shoto

Nansei-shoto

N

0   300km

0   150 miles

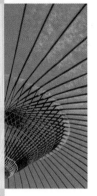

The land

The traveller in Japan cannot fail to be aware that this is a land of islands and mountains. You are never far from the sea, while inland you are surrounded by impenetrable mountains, with tiny villages tucked into the folds. Japan's geography has a powerful effect on the life of its people. The landscape is ever changing, shaken by earthquakes or moulded by volcanic eruptions.

Landscapes

The Japanese call their island country Nippon, 'the root of the sun' or 'the land of the rising sun'. There are 3,922 islands in all (but four main ones), stretching like a necklace towards the Asian mainland, off the coast of Korea and China. A long, narrow country, Japan extends from latitude 24°N to 45°N. Its northern part is parallel to Ottawa and Venice, the far south to Miami and the Sahara desert. From north to south it covers a distance of more than 3,000km (1,865 miles), but from east to west you are never more than an hour's drive from the sea.

The result is a dramatic variety of landscape. The northernmost of the major islands, Hokkaido, is a land of rolling pastures, wide-open plains, deep gorges and rugged volcanic mountains. Most people live on the central and largest island, Honshu. Mountain ranges, covered in deep forest, run like a spine right down the centre of the island. They offer spectacular views and fine skiing and hiking, but the land is largely uncultivable and uninhabitable. In the northwest is the Snow Country, a narrow coastal belt bordering the Sea of Japan, buried under snow 2–3m (6–10ft) deep for nearly half the year. The space left for living is very small. Most people live crammed together on the flat land along Honshu's east coast. This is where the major cities, industry and commerce are.

The islands to the south, Shikoku and Kyushu, are semi-tropical. Shikoku is a quiet backwater of terraced paddy fields, orange groves and coral reefs. Lush Kyushu is dominated by two brooding volcanoes, Mount Aso and Mount Sakurajima. Further south still lie Okinawa and the Ryukyu Islands, archetypal South Sea islands with white beaches and blue seas.

Restless earth

Geologically, Japan is a young country, still in the process of change. From north to south there are volcanoes, many of them live: Mount Fuji, dormant since 1707, still regularly spews smoke. Hot water, full of minerals, gushes from fissures in the rocks, forming natural hot springs. There are tremors nearly every day and from time to time a major earthquake such as the one that hit Kobe in 1995.

Climate

Because of Japan's latitude there are four distinct seasons, although large variations are experienced from north to south. Unless you are a skier or snowboarder, the best seasons to visit are spring and autumn. Spring, warm and dry, is cherry blossom time, while in late autumn everyone goes maple leaf viewing and the hills are a blaze of colour. Summer is hot and often humid (except in Hokkaido). Northern winters can be cold; elsewhere temperatures tend to stay above freezing (*see also p181*).

Limited land availability means every bit of space is utilised

History

10,000–300 BC Jomon period. Early inhabitants produce rope-impressed pottery.

300 BC–AD 250 Yayoi period. The Yayoi people develop rice cultivation and use bronze and iron implements.

AD 250–700 Kofun period. Large earthen tombs (*kofun*) built throughout Japan.

538–710 Asuka and Hakuho periods. Buddhism and Confucianism enter Japan from China.

710–94 Nara period. Nara becomes Japan's first capital. Flowering of culture.

794–1185 Heian period. Splendid new capital established in Kyoto (Heiankyo), which becomes the centre of an aesthetically refined aristocratic culture. Great advances in art, literature and religion. Murasaki Shikibu writes *The Tale of Genji* (*c.* 1010). But gradually civilisation becomes decadent.

1192–1333 Kamakura period. Military rule. Minamoto Yoritomo becomes first shogun, establishing court in Kamakura. The emperors, mere figureheads, remain cloistered in Kyoto while a succession of warlords battles for control.

1274 and 1281 Mongol armadas under Kublai Khan try twice to invade Japan but are driven back by a storm or divine wind (*Kamikaze*).

1336–1573 Ashikaga period. The Ashikaga shoguns rule from Kyoto. Building of Golden and Silver Pavilions, development of Noh theatre. Civil war overtakes the country.

1543 Portuguese sailors are shipwrecked in southern Kyushu, the first Europeans to reach Japan. They introduce bread, cake, Christianity and firearms.

1573–1600 Using Portuguese-style guns, Nobunaga Oda defeats his rivals but is assassinated by one of his own generals (1582). Toyotomi Hideyoshi succeeds him. Tokugawa Ieyasu defeats Hideyoshi's son at the Battle of Sekigahara (1600). Sen no Rikyu develops the tea ceremony.

1603–1868 Edo or Tokugawa period. Ieyasu makes himself shogun and ruler of all Japan. He moves his capital to Edo (Tokyo). The Tokugawa shoguns close the country to foreigners. The result is peace and a flowering of culture. Development of haiku poetry, kabuki and *bunraku* theatre and *ukiyo-e* woodblock prints.

1853 Matthew Perry, the American Commodore, steams into Yokohama Bay and demands that Japan open to trade with the West (commercial Treaty of Kanagawa signed 1854).

1868–1912 Meiji Restoration. The last shogun is ousted. Emperor Meiji leaves Kyoto to establish his capital in Edo, renamed Tokyo. His reign is a period of extraordinary modernisation. The Sino-Japanese War (1894–5) leads to a recognition of Korean independence and China cedes Taiwan to Japan.

1904–5 Russo-Japanese War. Japan defeats Russia – Asia's first modern defeat of a European power.

1905 Japan occupies Korea and annexes it in 1910.

1912–26 Taisho period. Reign of Emperor Taisho. The jazz age in Japan.

1914–18 World War I. Japan sides against Germany but is not deeply involved in the war and instead expands its economy, establishing a foothold in China.

1923 The Great Earthquake levels Tokyo. The city is quickly rebuilt.

1926–89 Showa period. Reign of Emperor Hirohito (posthumously known as Emperor Showa).

late 1920s– 1930s The world economic depression leads to the increase of nationalism and the military gradually takes power. In 1931 Japan invades Manchuria; in 1937 enters into a full-scale war with China. Japan, with its occupation of Korea, Taiwan and much of China, begins to build an empire.

1941   Japan attacks the US naval base at Pearl Harbor and enters World War II.

1945   Much of Tokyo destroyed. The Americans drop atomic bombs on Hiroshima and Nagasaki. For the first time in its history Japan is defeated.

1945–52   The Americans occupy Japan. New constitution (1946) gives more personal rights. Emperor renounces his divine descent.

1952   Occupation ends. Under the Liberal Democratic Party (LDP), Japan builds up its economy.

1964   Tokyo Olympics are held.

1965–92   Japan becomes an economic superpower.

1990– present   Heisei period. Reign of Emperor Akihito.

1993–6   The LDP loses power for the first time in 38 years. A succession of coalition governments follows. The leader of the Social Democrats becomes prime minister in 1994, leading a coalition dominated by the LDP.

1995   Massive earthquake devastates Kobe, Japan's fifth-largest city. The Aum Shinrikyo releases poison gas on the Tokyo subway, killing 12 and injuring hundreds.

2002   Japan co-hosts the FIFA World Cup with South Korea.

2002–3   North Korea's admission of a nuclear weapons programme and abduction of Japanese citizens in the 1960s and 1970s leads to high tension.

2004   Japanese combat troops sent to Iraq in the first deployment of Japanese troops since World War II.

September 2006   Prince Hisashito of Akishino is born, the first boy born into the royal family for 40 years.

2009   The centre-right Liberal Democratic Party, which had ruled for all but 11 months since 1955, loses general election to centre-left Democratic Party of Japan.

2010   The 1,300th anniversary of Japan's first capital, Nara.

Politics

The LDP (Liberal Democratic Party – conservative, despite the name) held power for nearly 40 years from 1955. Politics was a matter of infighting between rival factions within that party, with the other parties largely an irrelevance. Although it was superficially a democracy, in effect Japan functioned as a one-party state.

In 1993 the LDP finally fell from power and was replaced by a coalition government. Japan then had four prime ministers in the space of a year before the LDP once again took power in an unlikely coalition with the Japan Socialist Party. In 2009 the Democratic Party of Japan, a party founded in 1998, won a landslide election to take power for the first time.

Japan's system of government is close to the British model. At the top is the emperor, a purely constitutional monarch. Below him is the Diet, made up of two houses, like the British Parliament. Real decision-making power rests with the House of Representatives, elected every four years. The Upper House, known as the House of Councillors, is elected every six years.

The Iron Triangle

Power does not rest solely in the hands of politicians. The bureaucrats of key ministries, notably the Ministry of Finance and MITI (the Ministry of International Trade and Industry), wield much power. Big business forms the third side of the 'Iron Triangle'.

Despite its economic strength, Japan still plays only a small part in international affairs such as peace keeping. There are demands that it should contribute more. Japan's pacifist constitution, and its military relationship with the United States, provides much political friction.

The skyscrapers of Shinjuku, Tokyo

Samurai

Dotted around Japan are castles, potent symbols of its samurai past. Some are perched on hilltops; others guard the centre of cities, protected by moats and surrounded by a maze of streets to foil the enemy invader.

The first castles were built as fortresses for the warlords who battled to control Japan in the Middle Ages. Then the Tokugawa shoguns took power and decreed that there should be just one castle in each

Decorative samurai costume

province. This was where the daimyo – the warlord of the province – lived, though he was forced to make the long journey to Edo (Tokyo) every year to pay homage to the shogun.

The shoguns maintained peace by keeping strict control over the country. They divided society into four classes: samurai (warriors), peasant farmers, artisans and merchants. The samurai were not allowed to work, but were supported by the taxes of the farming class. They carried two swords and had the right to lop off the head of any member of the lower classes who failed to treat them with due respect.

With no battles to fight and no work to do, the samurai developed the fighting arts to a high level of skill, ceremonial and ritual. They also practised the tea ceremony, Zen meditation and Noh drama.

Many of Japan's most exquisite art forms were brought to a peak of refinement for the samurai. The curved Japanese sword is the finest in the world, combining strength and flexibility. Samurai also sported magnificent armour, including fearsome helmets adorned with horns and moustaches.

Only a few of the castles which stand today are originals. Most were destroyed during the early years of the Meiji era and in World War II and have been replaced by exact replicas, built in the post-war era. Nearly all contain a museum where the swords, armour, palanquins and treasures of the local daimyo are lovingly displayed.

The era of the samurai came to an end with the Meiji Restoration in 1868. With the Tokugawa shogunate defeated by the forces of Emperor Meiji, the former feudal lords (daimyo) were forced to give their lands to the emperor and by 1870 the samurai were consigned to history.

CODE OF HONOUR

A clear code of honour dictated the life (and death) of the samurai. Ritual suicide is an aspect of samurai culture that is its most dramatic expression. It was termed seppuku (known as hara-kiri in the West) – the act of slitting open one's belly, a privilege reserved for the samurai by which he could achieve posthumous fame. The origins of seppuku are uncertain but the first notable acts were performed in the 12th century. By the 17th century, the act of seppuku had become a fully developed ritual with Shinto undertones. Seppuku was performed for various reasons: in peacetime the penalty for striking another with a sword in anger was often suicide. Seppuku was also performed to follow one's shogun in death, to persuade one's shogun when all other reasoning had failed, and as atonement for a transgression. The last is possibly the best-known reason, which has been popularised far out of proportion to its frequency. Finally, it should be remembered that as ever-present as death may have been to many samurai, most died the old-fashioned way – of old age.

Culture

At a glance Japan seems like a mirror image of the West: modern people drive modern cars and walk along modern streets; there is a Disneyland®; McDonald's purveys burgers on every main street; and you can buy every imaginable variety of American ice cream. Yet it is strangely, undeniably different. The Japanese themselves are obsessed with their uniqueness. Barely a week goes by without a new book coming out on what it means to be Japanese.

The Japanese versus the rest

Until 1853, Japan was a closed society. Despite over 150 years of contact with the outside world, it is still very insular. You will soon discover that you are a *gaikokujin*, shortened to *gaijin*, an 'outside country person'. You are therefore an honoured guest. The Japanese tradition of hospitality is very strong and you will be treated with great kindness. But you will never be allowed to forget that you are different; even Westerners who speak perfect Japanese never cease to be *gaijin*.

All for one, one for all

Many people will tell you, 'We Japanese do this, we Japanese are like that . . .' The Japanese consider themselves primarily Japanese and only secondarily individuals. This does not mean that they have no individual thoughts and feelings. But in the last analysis they accept that their personal desires will often have to be put aside for the good of the group, be it their family, their company or society as a whole.

The dichotomy between doing your duty and your own desires is a fundamental theme in Japanese life and literature. A prime example is love. Most people still marry a suitable partner, approved of by their parents, and arranged marriages still occur. But a young person sometimes falls in love with someone completely 'unsuitable', and this can lead to tragedy.

Harmony

There is a Japanese saying: 'A nail that sticks up must be hammered down.' In a small island, crowded with people, the most important thing is to maintain harmony. As in many traditional societies, there are strict rules surrounding Japanese life. There is a well-ordered hierarchy: Japanese are expected to treat those above them with due respect and to follow their orders without questioning. Everyone – from the street cleaner to the head of a

THE CLOSED SOCIETY

In 1543 a group of Portuguese sailors, blown off course, landed on an island near Nagasaki. These were the first Westerners to arrive in Japan, quickly followed by others. The Japanese called the new arrivals *namban*, 'southern barbarians', and Nagasaki became the centre for all things Portuguese.

In 1600 Shogun Tokugawa Ieyasu of a newly unified Japan banned Christianity and sealed off the country. Only a few Dutch merchants were permitted to maintain a small trading post on Dejima (*see p141*).

For 220 years Japan remained closed until in 1853 the American Commodore Matthew C Perry steamed into Tokyo Bay and demanded that Japan open up to trade with the West. The shogun was overthrown. Emperor Meiji was established as titular head and Japan leapt into the modern age with dazzling speed.

multinational company – takes pride in their work and does the best they can.

Etiquette is very important. In almost any situation there is a proper way to behave. You take your shoes off at the door of the house; you bow when you meet someone, with the depth depending on their status. Rules like these maintain the surface harmony of society, and if the surface is harmonious, the rest of society will be too. The traditional Japanese arts, such as the tea ceremony, are all to do with establishing the form and getting it exactly right.

Breaking out

This does not mean that the Japanese do not have fun. For instance, in counterpoint to the Zen aesthetic of elegance and refinement, there are also exuberant Shinto festivals when everyone lets their hair down. In defiance of tradition, many young Japanese dress up in kitsch or Gothic clothing, or indulge in 'cosplay' and dress as anime characters, while the streets are decorated with plastic cherry blossoms or maple leaves (depending on the season) and the night is garish with glittering neon signs. In the subway, businessmen read pornographic comics . . . and the offerings of Japanese television are frequently bizarre.

After a hard day at the office obeying their superiors, men can go to the bar, get drunk, sit on the hostess's lap and tell their boss exactly what they think of him, without fear of repercussions. These are safety valves, accepted ways in which people can release all the pressure which their tight-knit society puts upon them.

A cosplay character

Festivals

Until you have seen a festival, a matsuri, *you have not seen Japan. Stripped down to loincloths, erstwhile clerks, businessmen and mechanics run through the streets, shouldering richly decorated palanquins that rest on huge wooden struts. Drums pound out an insistent beat, flutes tootle, dancers weave among the crowds, huge barrels of sake are smashed open. The most exciting festivals take place in summer. Tied to the harvest cycle, they are a way of propitiating and paying homage to the Shinto gods.*

January

Shogatsu (New Year) *31 December– 4 January*. This is the great festival of the year, when the whole country shuts down. At midnight bells ring out 108 times. People flock to their local shrine to strike the bell and wish for luck. In Tokyo, many people go to Meiji Shrine or Asakusa Kannon Temple. There is a wild Fire Festival at Mount Haguro (one of the three sacred mountains of Dewa) on New Year's Eve.

April

Hie Jinja Sanno Matsuri (Hie Shrine Sanno Festival) *14–15 April*. Twelve floats, flamboyantly carved and decorated, are pulled through the streets of the mountain city of Takayama. Look for the *karakuri* puppets which perform spectacular acrobatics.

Cherry Blossom Viewing *Mid- to late April*. The cherry blossom appears first in Okinawa; later, further north. There is much celebrating and sake-drinking under the trees. In Tokyo, go to Ueno Park; in Kyoto, to the gardens of Heian Shrine.

May

Kanda Matsuri *9–15 May, odd-numbered years*. One of the Big Three festivals, along with the Sanja Matsuri (*see below*) and Sanno Matsuri (*see June*). It features a parade of portable shrines and Shinto priests on horseback.

Aoi Matsuri (Hollyhock Festival) *15 May* in Kyoto. A procession of 500 people in Heian-period (794–1185) costume with horses and ox-carts winds from the Imperial Palace along the river to Kamigamo Shrine.

Sanja Matsuri *3rd Friday, Saturday, Sunday of May*. Downtown Tokyo celebrates around Asakusa Shrine, with more than 100 floats and huge crowds.

June

Sanno Matsuri *10–16 June, even-numbered years*. Around 300 people in costume parade through Tokyo to Hie Shrine in Nagatacho.

July

Gion Matsuri *14–17 July*. The most spectacular festival of all, held in Kyoto, it originated more than 1,000 years ago as a thanksgiving to celebrate the end of a plague. A procession of 32 floats, gorgeously decorated with dolls, statues, spears and lighted paper lanterns, winds through the city, accompanied by people in costume, dancers, gongs, drums and flutes.

Sumidagawa Fireworks *Late July*. A spectacular display in Tokyo.

August

Neputa *1–7 August*. Festival at Hirosaki in northern Honshu. Exquisite hand-painted floats illuminated from within depict mythical scenes.

Nebuta *2–7 August*. Neighbouring Aomori sees frenzied dancing in the streets and giant illuminated floats

A graphic image from a float, Neputa Festival

on which warriors battle with mythical monsters.

O-Bon *First half of August*. Important Buddhist festival when the whole of Japan comes alive with dancing in the streets, wonderful fireworks displays and tending of the ancestors' tombs. It is believed that the spirits of the dead come back to join the festivities.

Awa-Odori *12–15 August*. There's wild dancing in the streets of Tokushima, near Takamatsu, on Shikoku island.

Daimonji *16 August*. A fire festival at the end of O-Bon to see off the spirits of the dead. Beginning at 8pm, five huge bonfires are lit on the hills surrounding Kyoto, three depicting Chinese characters, one in the shape of a ship and one depicting a shrine gate.

October

Okunchi Festival *7–9 October*. In Nagasaki – Chinese dragon dances, floats and parades, accompanied by the clash of Chinese gongs, all commemorate ancient links with China.

Hachiman Matsuri *9–10 October*. Takayama's winter festival, akin to the April festival.

Mega Kenka Matsuri (Fighting Festival) *14–15 October*. In this wild, exciting festival in Himeji, youths in loincloths, carrying floats, charge each other until one float is smashed.

Jidai Matsuri (Festival of the Ages) *22 October*. Held in Kyoto, in which 2,000 people in ancient costumes parade from the Imperial Palace to Heian Shrine.

The art of the geisha

Along the lantern-lit streets of Gion or Pontocho, you might see a geisha or a *maiko* (a trainee geisha), flitting along like a butterfly in a colourful kimono, on high wooden clogs, face exquisitely painted. Do not imagine that a geisha is a prostitute. Geisha are ladies of the evening, not ladies of the night, trained in the arts of music and dancing, adept at charming shy Japanese males with their girlish conversation. Today, in Kyoto, young women still learn the art of the geisha, and geisha still entertain wealthy clients behind closed doors.

In Japanese, geisha means 'artist'. Geisha are professional hostesses who entertain customers in teahouses, *o-chaya*, by performing various traditional performance arts. A geisha's training takes many years during which they master many skills including performing the tea ceremony, traditional dance and singing, flower arranging, calligraphy and playing instruments such as the *shamisen* (a three-stringed lute).

This hidden life of geisha has led to many misconceptions about them in the West and to a certain extent in Japan also. Getting access to a teahouse is virtually impossible for all but the best-connected Japanese, but in Kyoto, many restaurants have begun hosting more casual *maiko* or geisha evenings.

Geisha are relatively new, dating back to the 18th century, but the geisha's role has existed for much longer. During the 7th century the *saburuko* (ones who serve) were a by-product of social displacements. Many women found themselves forced into a wandering lifestyle and in order to survive had to resort to prostitution. Although most of these women were from poor families, some were well educated and generally also skilled in singing, dance and social etiquette and as a result were often requested to entertain at aristocratic gatherings.

The *shirabyoshi*, who took their name from a traditional dance they performed, emerged during the late 11th century when many aristocratic families suffered a downturn in fortunes and the younger women became *shirabyoshi* to survive. They were known for their musical and dancing abilities. The *shirabyoshi* became accepted by Japanese high society and were supported by aristocratic families.

The modern-day geisha's origins date back to the 1750s when a new group of entertainers emerged from Kyoto and Osaka called *geiko* (these were originally men trained in the performing arts). In the early 1760s the first geisha were recognised and by the late 1780s a 'code of conduct' was written to govern where and how they could practise their trade.

The modern-day role of geisha is different from their historical roots. Today they are not prostitutes. It is acceptable for a geisha to have a patron, or *danna*, with whom they may be involved emotionally and sexually. Their main role is, however, that of an entertainer at banquets and parties. The geisha is usually accompanied by a *maiko*, a young geisha in training, who will, for example, perform a traditional dance while the geisha plays a *shamisen* and sings.

Although the number of geisha is declining, from around 90,000 in the 1920s to fewer than 10,000 today, their status as icons of high culture remains firm. The book *Memoirs of a Geisha* by Arthur Golden, and subsequent film, have increased interest in the ancient arts practised by members of this quintessentially Japanese profession.

A geisha's skills are reflected as much in her appearance as in her performance; a geisha's training includes flower arranging

Impressions

In some ways Japan is like a large village. It is a safe, orderly society where women can, in the main, confidently walk alone down the darkest street in the middle of the night, and where lost wallets are handed in to the police and returned to their owners. All this, along with trains that run precisely on time, makes Japan an extremely pleasant and comfortable place to visit.

Language

Your first shock on arriving in Japan may be the language: signs are written in seemingly incomprehensible characters. Fortunately you will also find many in English – station signs, for example.

Most Japanese educated after World War II have studied English for years, so while few people speak with fluency, most will understand you if you speak slowly and simply. If you are not understood, write your request down. Most people are far more used to reading English than to hearing it spoken. You will find most people eager to communicate, and learning a few simple Japanese words of politeness will make a big difference (*see pp186–7*).

Etiquette

Japan runs like clockwork – partly because there is a proper way to behave in practically any situation. As a foreigner, you will not be expected to know or follow these rules. But there are some faux pas that are simply unthinkable. The hints below may save embarrassment.

In the home

When visiting a Japanese home or a Japanese-style inn, remove your shoes at the door when you arrive: shoes are for outdoors only. You use slippers to walk around inside, but before entering a *tatami* (rice straw) matted room, remove these. *Tatami* is like furniture, used for sitting or sleeping, therefore you do not walk on it in slippers. At the toilet, remove your slippers, leave them outside the door and use the plastic toilet slippers.

When sitting on the floor, remember that the feet are considered unclean; avoid pointing them at people. The most formal way to sit is to kneel with your buttocks resting on your heels. This is, however, excruciatingly painful after a very short time, and nobody will be offended if you choose to sit cross-legged.

The bath

In Japan, the bath is a ritual and the ultimate relaxation, not just a question of cleanliness. The Japanese take a bath every evening, usually before dinner. The basic thing to remember is that everyone shares the bath water. Do not soil it with soap or dirt, and never pull the plug. Since a bath is for relaxation rather than cleansing, you will be expected to take a thorough shower before stepping into the tub. It will be extremely hot; sit still to avoid scalding and you will feel refreshed.

Mealtime etiquette

If you are dining with Japanese, you should say *itadakimasu* before you start eating and *gochisosamadeshita* to your host when you finish your meal. If you do not drink or do not want a particular sort of food, it is better to accept what is offered and not eat (or drink) it, rather than to make a fuss and refuse it.

Conversation

'Yes' (*Hai*) almost never means 'Yes, I agree'. It simply means 'Yes, I am listening'.

Other caveats

It is considered rude to sneeze or blow your nose in public; these noisy bodily functions are as offensive as belching. If it is unavoidable, turn aside and say 'Excuse me'.

Never express anger, no matter what the provocation. Always smile and remain calm. Shouting and throwing a tantrum is a sure sign of the barbarian foreigner. Effusive thanks and effusive apologies help to oil the wheels.

If you need to indicate something, gesture with the palm of the hand upwards. Never point.

Tea ceremony performed in a traditional teahouse

Getting around

Japanese public transport works with breathtaking efficiency. For longer distances most Japanese fly; in fact a return flight may work out cheaper than travelling by train. Trains are comfortable, extremely smooth, and they arrive so precisely on the dot that you can plan your schedule with split-second timing. Even the subways and buses follow timetables to the second.

Before you leave

The **Japan Rail (JR) Pass** is a must-buy if you plan to see more than Tokyo and Kyoto. The passes must be bought outside Japan, are valid only for foreign tourists, and allow unlimited travel on JR trains, including most bullet trains, JR buses and some ferries.

There are 7-, 14- and 21-day passes. Enquire at the Japan National Tourism Organization (JNTO; *see p189*).

Intercity travel

Air: There is an extensive network of internal airlines linking all major cities. The main domestic carriers are Japan Airlines (JAL), All Nippon Airways (ANA) and Japan Air Systems (JAS).
Rail: For all but the longest domestic trips, rail is the best option. Besides the JR lines, there are privately operated local lines, all equally punctual. There are many different categories of train, from local (*kakueki*) through semi-express (*kaisoku*) to express (*kyuko*) and sometimes super-express (*tokkyu*).

BULLET TRAINS

The aptly nicknamed bullet trains, or Shinkansen, hurtle through the country at speeds of up to 300kph (186mph). There are different types of train, and for the fastest travel you should look for the Nozomi or Hayate trains. Tickets can be open-ended (*jiyu-seki*) or assigned to a train and seat (*shitei-seki*). First-class carriages are known as Green Cars. While eating and drinking are considered bad manners on a regular train, the bullet trains serve snacks and drinks, and most travellers bring meals.

The two major routes: **Tokaido/San-yo** (Yokyo Hakata) – west from Tokyo through Kyoto, Osaka; **Tohoku** (Tokyo-Morioka) – north from Tokyo.

Non-Shinkansen trains run to the same cities. You'll pay between half and a third less, but expect to take twice as long.

A rechargeable magnetic Suica or PASMO card can be used on all trains, buses and most subway lines in Tokyo. Pay a ¥500 deposit for the card and you can then charge it in increments of ¥1,000. To find the best routes on Tokyo trains, visit *www.tokyo-subway.net*. An English-language railway timetable is available free from the JNTO.

If you have a JR Pass, you can make seat reservations free – advisable as trains are often full, particularly at peak seasons.

Driving

To hire a car you need an international driving licence. **Nippon Rentacar** (*tel: 03 3485 7196. www.freeroad.co.jp*), affiliated with Hertz, has a wide drop-off network. Reservations can be made from abroad.

Car rental starts at ¥7,000 for 24 hours. Try to hire a car with built-in GPS, which will direct you to your destination if you type in the phone number or the address. There is a very high toll to use the expressways.

Petrol is very expensive, costing approximately ¥900 per litre. The Japanese drive on the left and, except on expressways, very slowly. Beware of speed traps. The speed limit is 40kph (25mph) on all but major intercity roads, and the police fine offenders on the spot.

Hitch-hiking is not a Japanese custom, but Japan is one of the safest countries in the world in which to hitch (it is illegal to hitch-hike on expressways).

Local transport
Subways: Most major cities have extensive subway systems. Buy a ticket from a vending machine; if in doubt about the price, take the cheapest ticket and pay the excess at the other end. On the Tokyo subway you can use a Suica or PASMO card (*see* Rail, *opposite*).

Impressions

The super-fast bullet trains link most of the major cities on Honshu and Kyushu

Subways run from around 6am to around midnight. In rush hour, some lines operate women-only carriages, usually at the front or back of the trains. These carriages are clearly labelled in Japanese and English. Insert your personal information, provide a ¥500 deposit, and you will receive your card. You can add value of up to ¥10,000 at a time. Subways run until just after midnight.

Buses: Buses are complicated to use, but in some cities, such as Kyoto, they are the most efficient way of getting around. Free bus maps in Kyoto are easy to use. Some buses ask for the fare as you board (buses that you board at the front), while others ask you to take a ticket and pay as you leave (buses that you board at the rear). There is a change machine at the front of the bus.

Taxis: Don't expect your taxi driver to speak English or even to know where they are going. It is best to carry a note of the address of your destination in Japanese, to show the driver. A good idea is to get your hotel to print a map of your destination prior to getting in the cab.

Downtown Shinjuku at night

Fares are metered. There is no tipping. Taxi doors open and close automatically.

Trams: Many provincial cities, such as Hakodate, Kumamoto and Nagasaki, have trams. These are slow, noisy but very cheap and follow a clear route.

Bicycles: Cycling is an excellent way to get around small local areas. The law states that cyclists should use the road unless the pavement is marked as shared, though it's a rule almost universally ignored by cyclists and police alike.

When to go

The best seasons in Japan are spring and autumn (though every season has its attractions). Avoid New Year, Golden Week (29 April to 5 May) and the O-Bon holiday in early August, when many people return to their family home or go travelling.

At this time public transport is fully booked and crammed with passengers, the roads out of town are jammed, and Tokyo, the big city, becomes a ghost town.

Where to go

If you visit only Tokyo and Kyoto, you'll have an unforgettable trip. But if you have time to venture away from the Big Two, you'll find other faces of this beautiful country. Hokkaido offers world-class snow resorts as well as wild volcanic landscapes. Kyushu is the

---

THE INGENIOUS JAPANESE TOILET

In the countryside you will find some of the most primitive toilets you have ever seen, but Japan is also the land of the ultra-hi-tech toilet. Most modern homes have a computerised lavatory, with a heated toilet seat and a panel of buttons that operates the built-in bidet and blow-dry system. Ladies' toilets often have a machine that makes a loud flushing noise at the press of a button, drowning out other noises – a boon for the bashful. If you are seriously interested in toilets, Tokyo's INAX showroom has a constantly updated exhibition of the most state-of-the-art models.

---

home of shochu, the domestic distillate (*see box on p166*), as well as Fukuoka, often described as Japan's most livable city. It's a short hop from Kyoto to Nara, with some dazzling reminders of its brief spell as the country's capital, and there's also the oft-overlooked island of Shikoku, with picture-perfect paddy fields and orange groves. You could also do as the Japanese do, and relax in a hot-spring resort town.

Addresses in Japan

Only major roads have names so getting lost is normal, even for the Japanese. In an address, the city comes first, followed by the *chome* (district), *banchi* (city block) and then the *go* (house number). These are shown as 3 numbers, e.g. in Shibuya 5-5-3, the first 5 is the *chome*, and the 5-3 identifies the building in Shibuya. Most train stations have maps showing these numbers for the local area.

Tokyo and environs

Your first impression when you arrive in Tokyo will be of incredible life and energy. The streets throng with smart, fashionable people, glossy shops, expensive cars and new buildings. But this is only one face of Tokyo, the world's largest agglomeration and the 11th-largest city. Explore and you will find old neighbourhoods where the alleys are wide enough only for a bicycle; temples, shrines and gardens in the middle of bustling business districts. The best way to experience Tokyo is on foot: it's perfectly safe.

As a capital, Tokyo has a very short history. When Tokugawa Ieyasu (*see box on p74*) arrived in Edo in 1590, it was no more than a few fishing huts and a tumbledown castle. He ruled Japan from here as all-powerful shogun. In 1868, after the last shogun had been ousted, the Emperor Meiji moved to Edo, which was renamed Tokyo. The city has suffered fires, earthquakes and the fire bombing of World War II, so there are few historic monuments to be seen. But the spirit of old Edo is still alive.

NEIGHBOURHOOD TOKYO

Tokyo is a city of neighbourhoods, each with its own heart, its own logic and unique character. One of the best ways to get to grips with the city is to choose a neighbourhood and roam around it.

Akasaka

Akasaka's narrow streets are lined with bars, restaurants and nightclubs. The area is bordered by high-class hotels and the TBS television headquarters. The limousines that jam the streets do not stop at the bars but draw up at silent houses between them, hidden behind sand-coloured walls and closed gates. This is where the city's classiest geisha houses are located, where politicians, industrialists and their guests enjoy fine Japanese cuisine and the attentions of elegant geisha (*see pp18–19*).
Southwest of Imperial Palace.
Subways: Akasaka-mitsuke, Akasaka.

Akihabara

People say Akihabara is past its prime, for both electrical goods and geek culture, but it's still fun to spend an afternoon here.
Northeast Tokyo. Station: Akihabara.

Japan National Tourism Organization (JNTO)
Tokyo Kotsu Kaikan 10F, 2-10-1 Yurakucho, Chiyoda-ku Tokyo. Tel: 03 3201 3331.
Open: daily 9am–5pm.
  Located in Yurakucho, there is nothing to denote the fact that the TIC office is located here; just take the lift to the tenth floor.

Asakusa

Asakusa is the heart of old Edo, Tokyo's East End. In the days of the shogun, while the daimyo and samurai had their mansions in the hills now circled by the Yamanote rail line, Asakusa was where the merchants and craftsmen lived in humble homes. Here they developed a lively culture. Few of the old buildings survive, but the noisy, chaotic, downtown atmosphere remains.

Northeast Tokyo.

Subway: Asakusa; or by water bus from Hamamatsucho station or Hama Rikyu Gardens (see p36).

Ginza

Ginza is synonymous with glamour, sophistication and big-city living. Japan's most famous shopping district, the world's biggest brands have built architecturally dazzling flagship stores here, and many of the city's most exclusive restaurants have made Ginza their home. On Sundays the main street is closed to traffic.

10-minute walk southeast of Imperial Palace. Subway: Ginza.

Harajuku

Just behind Harajuku Station lies Meiji Jingu, Tokyo's most impressive Shinto shrine. Other than that, the area is all about novelty and fashion. Hot indie clothing stores and trendy cafés dominate the backstreets. Harajuku abuts Aoyama, home of big brand stores and landmark restaurants.

Southwest Tokyo. Station: Harajuku.

Ikebukuro

A mix of new and old Japan, Ikebukuro is one of Tokyo's main shopping and nightlife areas. It is notable for two huge shopping malls – Sunshine City (60 floors) and Seibu Loft (29 floors) – and one of the world's largest car showrooms (Toyota Amlux).

Northwest Tokyo. Station: Ikebukuro.

Odaiba

Built on reclaimed land in Tokyo Bay, this is one of Tokyo's top date spots, thanks to the night-time view across Tokyo Bay. Consequently, the area has

(Cont. on p30)

Shinjuku, Japan's Manhattan

Tokyo

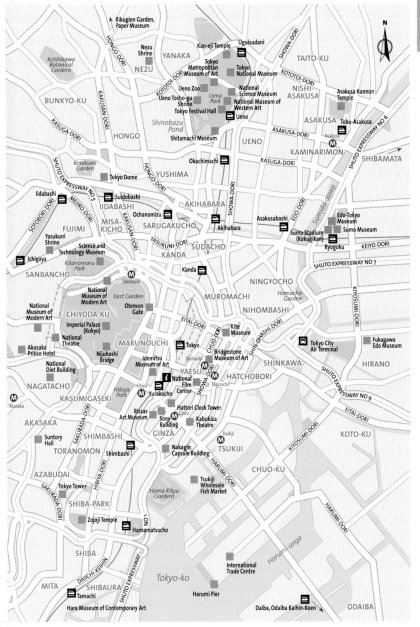

plenty of restaurants, Japan's largest Ferris wheel and the women-oriented Venus Fort shopping complex. But for all that, it can feel like a soulless place. *Station: Daiba.*

Roppongi

There are two faces to Roppongi. There's the rowdy nightlife, and there are the posher parts such as the Roppongi Hills and Midtown shopping complexes and a trio of major art galleries. Nearby Nishi-Azabu offers more sophisticated nightlife.
Southwest of the palace.
Subway: Roppongi.

Shibamata

A little-known but lovely area of old Tokyo, Shibamata is a long way from central Tokyo. It is well worth a visit, though, for its old-fashioned streets and sweet shops selling *dango* (round rice cakes filled with sweet bean jam) and other traditional Japanese sweets. After wandering the lanes, take a trip on the *Yagiri no Watashi* boat ride on the Edogawa River.
5-minute walk from Keisei Shibamata station on the Kanamachi line.

Shibuya

Tokyo's premier youth district is bright, brash and boisterous, and people either love or loathe it. If you can tolerate the cacophony, it offers cheap eats, affordable shopping and some of the best people-watching opportunities in the city.
West Tokyo. Station: Shibuya.

Shinjuku

Shinjuku's two wildly contrasting faces epitomise the extremes of Tokyo living. On the west of the tracks is Japan's answer to Manhattan, full of gleaming modern skyscrapers, dominated by Kenzo Tange's granite-and-glass City Hall. Cross to the east side and you find yourself in a warren of streets crammed with shops and boutiques. Leave the main road and you plunge into the seedy alleys of **Kabukicho**, with strip joints, massage parlours and plenty more. This being Japan, the area is not dangerous, though it is sensible to be a little wary if you wander there at night.
West Tokyo. Station: Shinjuku.

Tsukiji Fish Market

A huge and chaotic place that feeds Tokyo's insatiable demand for anything that comes from the sea. About 2,500 tonnes (2,460 tons) of fish pass through the market each day. Arrive before 8am and visit the middlemen's market. There is always something to see. Wear old shoes.
Central Tokyo. Subway: Tsukiji.

Ueno

Ueno is a gritty area, largely untouched by big chains. The Ameyoko market and nostalgic eateries ooze local charm, while the vast Ueno Park boasts many of the capital's top museums. **Yanaka**, to the north of Ueno, is one of the best-preserved parts of old Tokyo.
Northeast Tokyo. Station: Ueno.

Modern architecture in Tokyo

Tokyo is an architect's dream. Modest planning regulations, a local appetite for spectacle, and a shelf-life of a couple of decades for most buildings has resulted in a cityscape that is dazzling, innovative and thoroughly discordant.

The Prada building in Minami-Aoyama

Outstanding architects such as Kenzo Tange, Kisho Kurokawa and Tadao Ando have all made their marks on the capital (see Tange's Yoyogi Olympic Stadium, Kurokawa's National Art Center, Tokyo, and Ando's 21_21 Design Sight for examples) but the turn of the century saw foreign architects and fresh Japanese faces contribute to the thrilling mosaic of Tokyo.

Kengo Kuma is perhaps the leader of the new generation of Japanese architects, and you can see his handiwork in the form of Aoyama's Nezu Museum and Tiffany & Co.'s Ginza flagship. The other luxury megabrands have also built dazzling Ginza stores, with Swarovski turning to Tokujin Yoshioka, Louis Vuitton using Jun Aoki, and Mikimoto also hiring Jun Aoki.

The foreign architects had their say, too, with Renzo Piano providing Hermès with its Ginza store, and Herzog & de Meuron designing the much-praised Prada store in Aoyama.

It is not an aesthetically harmonious city, but it is a great place to see some truly inventive architecture.

Tokyo transport

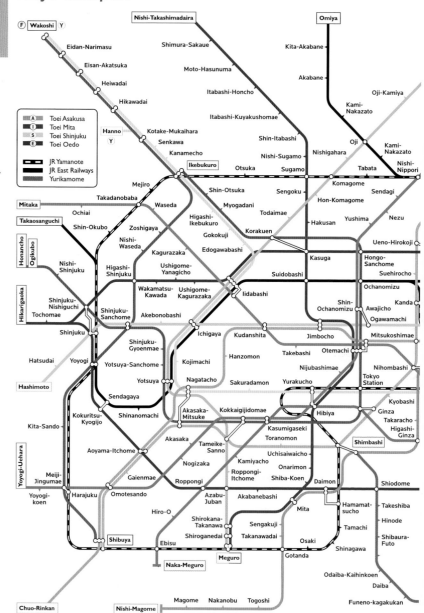

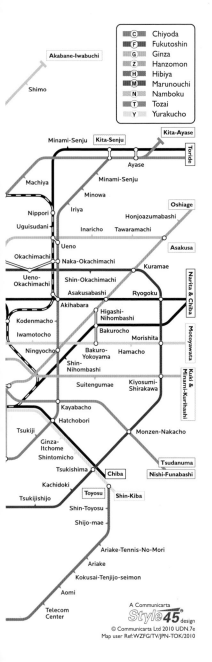

C	Chiyoda
F	Fukutoshin
G	Ginza
Z	Hanzomon
H	Hibiya
M	Marunouchi
N	Namboku
T	Tozai
Y	Yurakucho

A Communicarta
Style 45 design
© Communicarta Ltd 2010 UDN.7e
Map user Ref:WZFG/TV/JPN-TOK/2010

TRAVELLING IN TOKYO SUBWAYS

Most of Tokyo's train lines are operated by either private company Eidan or government-owned Toei. There are several ways to purchase tickets, but the easiest is to buy a PASMO or Suica rechargeable card. If buying individual tickets, you can purchase the cheapest fare and pay the difference at the yellow 'fare adjustment' machines at your destination.

For an up-to-the-minute timetable of the JR and subway lines, visit *www.hyperdia.com*. Subway lines predominate with two major exceptions; the **JR Yamanote** and **Chuo** lines. The first is particularly useful as it forms a ring around central Tokyo enclosing the majority of its attractions.

Look for the useful English maps posted around.

A crowded train

Japanese gardens

Garden design has a long history in Japan and is considered a high art form. The art forms of Japan are distinctive for their use and appreciation of abstract and minimalist forms and these traditions are also to be found in the gardens of Japan.

Japanese gardens are most commonly associated with *kare sansui*, sometimes called Zen gardens. Zen gardens are a celebrated expression of the Zen way. Stark and tranquil, they consist simply of ambiguously shaped rocks set in a bed of raked gravel. Such gardens are

Ablaze with the colours of autumn

A garden meant for contemplation

often tiny – yet they contain a world of meaning. Zen gardens were designed for monks to gaze at in contemplation. They invite the viewer to sit and look; the more you contemplate the more the depths of meaning emerge.

Japanese gardens are highly refined miniaturisations of the Japanese landscape. *Tsukiyama* gardens invariably feature a path that takes the viewer through a series of scenes. This separation is achieved by the use of concealing features or the deliberate slowing of the viewer's pace, by using stepping stones or rougher paving, when the viewer reaches an area deserving more detailed attention. A common theme of these scenes is an attempt to incorporate the distant landscape into the garden by, for example, framing a particular view of a mountain.

The *chaniwa*, tea garden, is another common type of Japanese garden. As well as providing an artistic backdrop for the tea ceremony, it also provides a water feature in the garden to rinse hands and mouth.

With the opening of Japan to the West in the 19th century, many of the ideas found in Japanese gardens found their way abroad, and the influence of Japan can be seen in the design of both municipal parks and household gardens.

GARDENS AND PARKS

Tokyo contains several exquisite landscaped gardens that are a legacy of the rule of the shoguns, when every daimyo (feudal lord) had to maintain a mansion in Edo (old Tokyo). Besides the gardens described below, other oases of green include the Imperial Palace East Garden and Meiji Shrine Outer Garden (*see p43*), and Yoyogi Park (*see p48*).

Also see: www.tokyo-park.or.jp/english

A perfect magnolia flower on display in the poetic Rikugien Garden

Hama Rikyu Onshi-Teien (Hama Rikyu Gardens)

These beautiful gardens border the Sumida River. They once belonged to the shoguns and later to the Imperial family. Winding paths leading to tiny hillocks circle a small lake. A central island houses a pavilion and small teahouse, close to both the Tsukiji Fish Market and Ginza. You can also join the Sumida River cruise to and from Asakusa from inside the gardens.

10-minute walk south of Shimbashi station. Tel: 03 3541 0200.
Open: Tue–Sun 9am–4.30pm (last entry 4pm). Admission charge.

Rikugien Garden

Rikugien's gravelled paths meander around a lake, crossed with bridges and overhung with exquisitely trimmed pine trees. Designed and laid out by the daimyo Yoshiyasu Yanagisawa around 1700, the garden re-creates 88 scenic spots mentioned in Chinese and Japanese literature.

10-minute walk south of Komagome station. Tel: 03 3941 2222.
Open: Tue–Sun 9am–4.30pm (last entry 4pm). Admission charge.

Shinjuku Gyoen (Shinjuku Imperial Gardens)

The rolling lawns of Shinjuku Gyoen are a great place to relax on hot summer days. Once the estate of a daimyo family, it was made into a park in the Meiji period, when Japan was absorbing many influences from the West. Besides the Western-style lawns, there are lakes, a Japanese garden with a teahouse, a pond with giant carp, and a formal French landscape garden with rose beds and clipped hedges.

5-minute walk south of Shinjuku Gyoenmae subway. Tel: 03 3350 0151.
www.env.go.jp/garden/shinjukugyoen/ english/index.html. Open: Tue–Sun 9am–4.30pm (last entry 4pm). Admission charge.

Ueno Koen (Ueno Park)

Tokyo's oldest and largest park was based on Le Bois de Boulogne in Paris. It also includes a zoo and several excellent museums, including the Tokyo National Museum and the Tokyo Metropolitan Museum of Art. The Bentendo temple is one of many worth visiting. The park is popular for *hanami* (cherry blossom viewing parties) during the cherry blossom season, when it becomes very crowded.

1-minute walk north of Ueno station. Tel: 03 3828 5644. Free admission.

MUSEUMS

Tokyo is a treasure trove of museums. There are the huge public collections such as the Tokyo National Museum, the finest collection of Japanese art in the world; tiny museums lovingly devoted to just one thing, such as swords, kites or paper; and many fine and idiosyncratic collections assembled by business magnates who invested their fortunes in art. Several fascinating museums are devoted to the history of Edo, with streets of wooden buildings and audio-visual evocations of Edo life taking you back to old Tokyo.

Edo-Tokyo Hakubutsukan (Edo-Tokyo Museum)

This splendid museum opened in March 1993. In the heart of downtown Tokyo, next to the sumo stadium, it celebrates the life and history of the city of Tokyo, from its founding in the 16th century to the present. You enter via a replica of Nihombashi (the Bridge of Japan, from where every distance in Japan is measured) and walk between full-scale models of old Edo/Tokyo buildings – a kabuki theatre, a newspaper office, shops and homes. There are displays devoted to samurai,

The Edo-Tokyo Museum displays the history of Tokyo

townspeople, the pleasure quarters, the great earthquake and the war.
At Ryogoku station. Tel: 03 3626 9974. www.edo-tokyo-museum.or.jp. Open: Tue–Sun 9.30am–5.30pm (till 7.30pm Sat). Admission charge.

Ghibli Museum

The museum devoted to the award-winning works of Hayao Miyazaki has enough to entertain fans. Tickets must be purchased in advance at one of the outlets listed on the website.
15-minute walk from Mitaka station. Tel: 05 7005 5777. www.ghibli-museum.jp. Open: Wed–Mon 10am–6pm. Admission charge.

Hara Museum of Contemporary Art

The Hara is devoted to contemporary art. Founded by Toshio Hara in 1979, it occupies his striking 1938 Bauhaus-style family residence. There are several major exhibitions a year, showcasing leading Japanese and international artists of the stature of Christo Javacheff (the New York artist famous for his 'wrapped buildings'), and an annual spring show of work by young Japanese artists. In the garden is a café designed by world-famous architect Arata Isozaki.
10-minute walk west of Kita-Shinagawa station, 15-minute walk south of Shinagawa station. Tel: 03 3445 0651. www.haramuseum.or.jp. Open: Tue–Sun 11am–5pm (till 8pm Wed). Closed: Mon & while changing exhibitions. Admission charge.

Idemitsu Bijutsukan (Idemitsu Museum of Art)

This museum houses one of the finest collections of classical Japanese and Chinese art in Tokyo, acquired by the oil tycoon Sazo Idemitsu (though only a small selection is on display at any one time). It includes superb examples of Chinese and Japanese ceramics, ancient screens and painted scrolls, lacquerware and bronzes. Idemitsu's particular passion was for the wild, inspired ink paintings of the 17th-century Zen artist Sengai: the museum owns nearly all in existence. It also has one of the best views in Tokyo, right over the Imperial Palace.
5-minute walk from Yurakucho subway, 10-minute walk north of Hibiya subway, Yurakucho station. Tel: 03 5777 8600 or 03 3213 9402. www.idemitsu.co.jp. Open: Tue–Sun 10am–5pm (till 7pm Fri). Admission charge.

Kagaku Gijutsukan (Science and Technology Museum)

This is a hands-on science museum where visitors can interact with every exhibit, the perfect place to take children on a rainy day. They can ride in a spaceship, an earthquake simulator or a time machine, play with new computer programs and learn about iron, energy, plastics or electricity.
10-minute walk west of Takebashi subway. Tel: 03 3212 8544. www.jsf.or.jp. Open: daily 9.30am–4.50pm (last entry 4pm). Admission charge.

Kami no Hakubutsukan (Paper Museum)

The Chinese invented paper, but the Japanese turned it into an artform: craftsmen create *washi*, exquisitely fine paper made from mulberry bark; paper is folded to make origami; and doors and windows of traditional houses are made from paper. The Paper Museum celebrates all these.

2-minute walk from Oji station.
Tel: 03 3916 2320. www.papermuseum.jp.
Open: daily 10am–5pm (last entry 4pm).
Admission charge.

Kokuritsu Bijutsukan (National Museum of Modern Art, Tokyo)

The National Museum of Modern Art, Tokyo was Japan's first national art museum, opening in 1952. It consists of an art museum and crafts gallery in Kitanomaru Koen, close to the Imperial Palace, and the National Film Center, which is in Kyobashi, near Ginza. The art museum houses works from the Meiji and Taisho periods through to contemporary pieces from the 1970s onwards. The focus is on Japanese art in the context of global modern art. The Crafts Gallery contains Japanese and local crafts in genres such as ceramic, glass, metal, wood, bamboo and lacquer work, as well as dolls and industrial and graphic design, from the Meiji period to the present day.

The National Film Center is dedicated to preserving and researching film – both national and international. It is a member of the Fédération Internationale des Archives du Film and hosts regular screenings at 3pm and 7pm Tuesday to Friday.

Art Museum and Craft Gallery. 5-minute walk southwest of Takebashi subway.

Tokyo and environs

The entrance to the Mori Art Museum

Open: Tue–Thur, Sat & Sun 10am–5pm (last entry 4.30pm), Fri 10am–8pm (last entry 7.30pm). Admission charge. The National Film Center. 1-minute walk southeast of Kyobashi subway, 1-minute walk west of Takaracho subway. Tel: 03 5777 8600. www.momat.go.jp. Open: daily 11am–6.30pm (last entry 6pm). Admission charge.

Kokuritsu Kagaku Hakubutsukan (National Science Museum)

Five large halls are devoted to all kinds of science. There are dinosaurs and a section on the evolution of the Japanese people, as well as a working model of the 'maglev', the futuristic magnetically levitated railway, and a flight simulator where you can try out your skills as a pilot.
5-minute walk north of Ueno station. Tel: 03 3822 0111. www.kahaku.go.jp. Open: Tue–Sun 9am–5pm (till 8pm Fri). Admission charge.

Mori Art Museum

The Mori Art Museum (MAM) is located at the top of the Mori Tower in Roppongi and has breathtaking views of the city from the museum on the 53rd floor and from the Tokyo City View observation deck. It's a world-class art museum that stages ambitious and imaginative exhibitions of Japanese and international works in all media. If you only have time for one gallery, make it this one.
1-minute walk southwest of Roppongi subway. Tel: 03 5777 8600. www.mori. art.museum. Open: Wed–Mon 10am– 10pm (last entry 9.30pm), Tue 10am–5pm (last entry 4.30pm). Admission charge.

National Art Center, Tokyo

The beautiful glass construction that houses the National Art Center is almost more interesting than the museum itself. It was designed by Kisho Kurokawa to maximise energy saving through its undulating shape. While this 14,000sq-m (150,695sq-ft) space deliberately does not house a permanent exhibition, it regularly runs a series of different contemporary exhibitions – anything from contemporary Japanese photography to Vermeer.
1-minute walk south of Nogizaka subway, 5-minute walk northwest of Roppongi subway (Oedo and Hibiya lines). Tel: 03 6812 9900. www.nact.jp. Open: Mon, Wed, Thur, Sat & Sun 10am–6pm (last entry 5.30pm), Fri 10am–8pm (last entry 7.30pm). Admission charge.

Nihon Mingeikan (Japan Folk Crafts Museum)

This is a wonderful collection of folkcrafts – stoneware pots, indigo-dyed fabrics, heavy wooden furniture – assembled by the folk-art patron and author Yanagi Soetsu, and lovingly displayed in a fine old farmhouse, brought piece by piece from the country and reconstructed here.
10-minute walk northwest of Komaba Todaimae station. Tel: 03 3467 4527. www.mingeikan.or.jp. Open: Tue–Sun 10am–5pm (last entry 4.30pm). Admission charge.

Ota Kinen Bijutsukan
(Ota Memorial Museum of Art)

This small, tranquil museum in the heart of noisy Harajuku houses a fine collection of *ukiyo-e* (Japanese woodblock prints), assembled by the business tycoon Seizo Ota. The 12,000 works include many by Hokusai, Hiroshige and other masters of the art. Only a few are on show at any one time.
5-minute walk from Meiji Jingumae subway. Tel: 03 3403 0880. www.ukiyoe-ota-muse.jp. Open: Tue–Sun 10.30am–5.30pm (last entry 5pm). Closed: Mon & 27th to end of each month. Admission charge.

Shitamachi Fuzoku Shiryokan
(Shitamachi Museum)

This is the first of the museums built to preserve the flavour of old Edo/Tokyo (Shitamachi means 'downtown'). On the ground floor are old shops and houses, including a merchant's house and a sweet shop; upstairs is a jumble of utensils, toys and knick-knacks.
5-minute walk south of Ueno station and subway. Tel: 03 3823 7451. Open: Tue–Sun 9.30am–4.30pm. Admission charge.

Sumo Hakubutsukan
(Sumo Museum)

Sumo enthusiasts will not want to miss this sumo hall of fame, next to the Kokugikan, the sumo stadium, where you can admire the champions' embroidered trappings and look at woodblock prints of past heroes.
2-minute walk north of Ryogoku station. Tel: 03 3622 0366. Open: Mon–Fri 10am–4.30pm. Free admission.

Syabi (Tokyo Metropolitan
Museum of Photography)

This museum showcases Japanese and international photography, as well as hosting short film festivals.

The spectacular National Art Center opened in 2007

Tokyo and environs

7-minute walk east of Ebisu JR station.
Tel: 03 3280 0099. www.syabi.com. Open:
Tue, Wed, Sat & Sun 11am–6pm, Thur &
Fri 10am–8pm. Admission charge.

Tokyo Kokuritsu Hakubutsukan (Tokyo National Museum)

You can get some idea of the incredible
wealth, variety and tradition of
Japanese art and culture from the
89,000 items here, the best collection in
the world. The main building is
devoted to superb examples from every
field of Japanese art: painting, from
ancient mandalas to woodblock prints;
sculpture, including 7th- and 8th-
century Buddhas and modern works;
ceramics, textiles, swords, lacquerware,
inro (medicine boxes) and exquisitely
carved *netsuke* (belt toggles).

Don't miss the magnificent
collection of prehistoric and proto-
historic art in the Meiji-period
Hyokeikan building, including Jomon-
period earthenware, bug-eyed figurines
and *haniwa*, terracotta images of
people, houses and animals from
tomb burials.

Tokyo's oldest temple, Asakusa Kannon

10-minute walk north of Ueno station.
Tel: 03 3822 1111. Open: Tue–Sun
9.30am–5pm (last entry 4pm).
Admission charge.

TEMPLES AND SHRINES
Asakusa Kannon Temple

Asakusa Kannon-do (also known as
Senso-ji) preserves the flavour of old
Tokyo. The temple, Tokyo's oldest and
best loved, was founded in 628 when
two brothers reportedly found a golden
image of Kannon, the deity of
compassion, in their fishing nets. This
is no solemn house of worship. Pass
Kaminarimon (Thunder Gate), with its
twin gods of thunder and wind, and you
come to Nakamise-dori, a noisy arcade
jammed with pilgrims, visitors and
shopkeepers, which leads north to the
main temple compound. The temple
courtyard is lined with fortune-telling
booths. In front of the temple is a large
incense cauldron. Visitors waft the
smoke against their body, believing it
will deliver good health. The vast temple,
a post-war reconstruction, houses the
statue of Kannon, hidden within a
gold-plated shrine (*see also p46*).
*10-minute walk north of Tobu-Asakusa
station. Tel: 03 3842 0181. Open: daily
6am–5pm. Grounds always open.
Free admission.*

Kokyo (Tokyo Imperial Palace)

The Imperial Palace is the still centre at
the heart of Tokyo. The home of the
emperor and his family, the palace
itself is hidden deep inside a large,

impregnable expanse of woods and gardens. The public may enter only twice a year: at New Year (2 Jan, 9.30am–3pm) and on the emperor's birthday (23 Dec, 8.30–11am), when the emperor waves to the crowds.

This is where Tokyo began. The shogun built his castle here and the city expanded around it. The site of the castle is now the **East Garden** (**Higashi Gyoen**), which is open to the public. Some guardhouses and fortified turrets remain, together with the massive ramparts, built with huge slabs of volcanic rock shipped from Izu, 100km (62 miles) away. The most famous view from the East Garden is across Nijubashi Bridge to Fushimi Tower. Or look down into the grounds from the observation floor of the nearby 36-storey Kasumigaseki Building.

2-minute walk west of Otemachi subway. East Garden. Open: Mar–mid-Apr & Sept–end Oct Tue–Thur, Sat & Sun 9am–4.30pm (last entry 4pm); mid Apr–end Aug Tue–Thur, Sat & Sun 9am–5pm (last entry 4.30pm); Nov–early Feb Tue–Thur, Sat & Sun 9am–4pm (last entry 3.30pm). Closed early–end Feb. Free admission.

Meiji Jinju (Meiji Shrine)

Meiji Shrine is dedicated to Emperor Meiji, who presided over Japan's transformation from feudal country to modern state. The shrine was completed in 1920, as a memorial to both him and his empress. You enter via one of the largest wooden *torii* (gateway to a

Shinto shrine) in the country, and stroll along shady paths to the shrine buildings, rebuilt to the original design in 1958 after World War II destruction. In the grounds is the **Iris Garden** (**Meiji Jingu-gyoen**), where the Imperial couple used to stroll; it is not to be missed in June when more than 100 varieties of iris bloom. In the first three days of January, millions of people visit to make their New Year wishes.

Harajuku station or Meiji Jingumae subway.
Inner garden (tel: 03 3379 5511) and shrine. Open: daily dawn–dusk. Free admission.
Iris Garden. Open: Mar–early Nov daily 9am–5pm (till 4pm in winter). Admission charge.

Ueno Tosho-gu-Jinja (Ueno Tosho-gu Shrine)

Tucked away in a quiet corner of Ueno Park (*see p37*), behind the zoo, is a shrine to Shogun Tokugawa Ieyasu, who unified Japan and founded Tokyo, and whose family dominated the country for 250 years. Completed in 1651, it is in the same lavish style as the Toshogu Shrine at Nikko (*see pp74–5*) and is the only shrine in Tokyo designated a 'National Treasure'. The dragons carved on the gateposts and the animal paintings within the shrine are by famous 17th-century artists.

10-minute walk west of Ueno station. Tel: 03 3822 3455. Open: daily 9am–6pm. Admission charge.

The emperors

The origin of the Japanese emperors is intertwined with Japanese mythology, which says that Jimmu ascended to the throne in 660 BC. He was a descendant of one of the children of the first two gods in Japan's creation myth. When he became the first emperor, the sun goddess gave him the Three Treasures (a mirror, sword and beads) that act as symbols of the emperor's authority.

The Imperial household recognises 125 legitimate monarchs, starting with Jimmu, but most historians regard the first 14 as mythical figures. Bidatsu (AD 539–72) is widely considered the first true emperor.

Since the 6th century the Japanese emperors have used the title Tenno (heavenly sovereign) or Tenshi (the son of heaven). Both these terms are gender neutral in Japanese, and Japan in its history has had six female emperors, although none of them passed the throne on to their offspring.

The first permanent capital was built in AD 710 in Heijo-kyo (Nara). In 794 it was relocated to Heian-kyo (Kyoto) and the Imperial family resided here until 1686 (when they moved to Tokyo). From the start the Imperial family's political power started to decline, until by the 9th century actual power rested with military families (shogunates). Although for most of Japan's history the emperor's actual power was symbolic, or at best limited, all actual rulers were keen on having Imperial legitimisation for their position as rulers of Japan.

With the Meiji Restoration of 1868, the Tokugawa shogunate was overthrown, the Emperor Meiji became the head of state and the Imperial family moved to Tokyo. Although the emperor's power was theoretically absolute, actual power eventually ended up in the hands of the generals and admirals in Japan's military. The new government launched a rapid series of reforms aimed at modernising the largely agrarian economy and the strict system of social hierarchy. A by-product of this modernisation was the prospering of state-supported industries, especially the large family businesses called *zaibatsu*, which held considerable influence.

Japan wrote its first Western-style constitution in 1889 and a parliament, the Diet, was established, with the

Moats and high walls surround the Imperial Palace

emperor keeping sovereignty. During this period there was a revival of nationalistic feelings, and the worship of Shinto and the emperor was emphasised and taught in educational institutions. The post-war constitution of 1946 states that the emperor has only a symbolic function and he (Hirohito) renounced his claim of divine origins.

Hirohito's son, Akihito, became emperor on 7 January 1989, and is married to Michiko, the first empress not to come from the nobility. His eldest son's daughter is adored by the Japanese public and, until the birth of Prince Akishino and Princess Kiko's son on 6 September 2006, there was a growing opinion that the constitution should be redrawn to allow her eventually to become Japan's seventh female emperor.

Walk: Downtown Tokyo

This stroll through the heart of old Tokyo takes in the city's oldest and best-loved temple and also one of the brashest symbols of the modern city. Bear in mind that Dembo-in Garden closes at 3pm.

Allow 3 to 5 hours.

Start at Hama Rikyu Gardens, near Shimbashi station. If time is short, begin at Azuma Bridge (subway: Asakusa).

1 Hama Rikyu Gardens

At Hama Rikyu Gardens (*see p36*), board the water bus which departs about every 40 minutes for Asakusa to go up the River Sumida, past modern high-rise buildings crammed next to wooden temples and geisha houses. Finally to your right you see Philippe Starck's gleaming Flamme d'Or.

Alight at Azuma Bridge.

2 Azuma-bashi (Azuma Bridge)

Before starting your walk, admire the outrageous Flamme d'Or, a beer hall and restaurant built for the Asahi beer company.

Cross the main road in front of you and take the covered shopping street. On your right is a gateway, Kaminarimon.

3 Nakamise-dori (Nakamise Street)

Kaminarimon (Thunder Gate), a reconstruction of the original, which burnt down in 1865, bears the thunder god (right) and the wind god (left).

Walk through into Nakamise-dori, lined with stalls selling anything from trinkets to happi coats (blue cotton workmen's jackets), oiled umbrellas and freshly baked rice crackers.

At the end of Nakamise-dori you come to another great gateway, Hozomon, and Asakusa Kannon Temple.

4 Asakusa Kannon (Senso-ji) Temple

After exploring the temple and its grounds (*see p42*), visit the Asakusa-jinja (shrine) behind the main temple. This 17th-century Shinto shrine was built to honour the brothers who discovered the Kannon statue.

Retrace your steps down Nakamise-dori and take the first turning on the right. To your right is a gate leading to Dembo-in.

5 Dembo-in

A peaceful retreat, Dembo-in is the residence of the abbot of Asakusa Kannon. The 17th-century garden with its large pond, home to many turtles, has beautiful views of the five-storey pagoda (not open to the public).

Continue along the road to your right to a wide street (Shushiya-dori) lined with cinemas, strip joints and game parlours. Japan's first cinema was built here in 1903, and people flocked to see movies, cabaret and music-hall. *Return via the shopping arcades to Asakusa station, or stroll on to the Moorish towers of Hanayashiki playground. Walk through the arcade,*

then cross the main road, turn right down the first side road and cut through the backstreets towards a small temple.

6 Matsuchiyama-shoten

Dedicated to marital bliss and prosperity, this is where young blades would wait for the boat to the pleasure quarters.
Open: Mon–Sat 6am–4.30pm.
Free admission.
Return to Asakusa subway along the river.

Walk: Downtown Tokyo

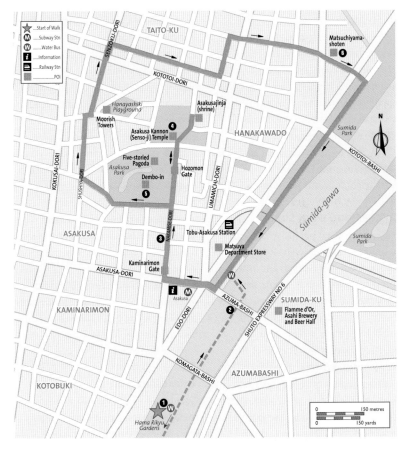

Walk: Modern Tokyo

This walk takes you through some of the city's busiest and most fashionable streets. It is full of interest any day of the week but best on Sundays, when Harajuku is at its brightest and busiest.

Allow 3 hours.

At Shibuya station, take the Hachiko exit.

1 Shibuya

Look out for the statue of Hachiko the dog in the station square. The real Hachiko waited patiently every day at the station for 11 years after his master died until his own death in 1936, the perfect example of the faithful dog. Roads radiate in every direction.

Cross the road and walk north past Seibu department store. Turn left on to Koen-dori, opposite Marui Young store.

2 Koen-dori (Park Street)

Park Street is full of chic young people sauntering up and down. Turn left at the first major crossroads and you'll come to Tokyu Hands, a store that seems to sell everything, a perfect place to pick up Japanese souvenirs. The small backstreets behind Parco are worth exploring too. The top of the street opens on to the magnificent Yoyogi Olympic Stadium (*see p31*).

Cross the road and walk straight on, the stadium to your right. At the end of the road turn right along Yoyogi Park.

3 Inogashira-dori (Yoyogi Koen Perimeter Road)

This street runs along the side of Yoyogi Park, one of Tokyo's largest. On fine Sundays you can see all kinds of Tokyo subcultures, including bequiffed Teddy boys in winkle-pickers and black leather, gyrating to some old-time rock'n'roll. Further on, at the entrance to the Meiji Shrine, at the weekend you will find the *cosplay-zoku* (costume play gang). Teenage girls from Tokyo's sleeper towns pose, for photographers and bemused tourists, wearing Gothic make-up and a mixture of arch-vamp/cartoon nurse exaggeration.

At the end of the road turn left to explore Meiji Shrine (see p43). Leave by the same gate. Turn left to pass Harajuku station then take the small road to your right, opposite the second station exit.

4 Takeshita-dori

Takeshita-dori is crammed with Tokyo's teenagers shopping for second-hand threads or pet costumes.

Turn right at the end of Takeshita-dori and walk along Meiji-dori to the main intersection. Turn right here and right again for Ota Memorial Museum of Art (see p41) or left on to Omotesando.

5 Omotesando-dori

Omotesando-dori is the epitome of chic Tokyo. This broad, tree-lined boulevard was built at the time of the Tokyo Olympics in 1964. Stroll past expensive boutiques and elegant street cafés. On the right, look for the Oriental Bazaar and Kiddyland (*see p151*), and some playful architecture from big brands such as Tod's and Louis Vuitton.

The tour ends at Omotesando subway station. If you're feeling energetic, carry on straight across the traffic lights into the Aoyama area, where Tokyo's world-famous fashion designers have boutiques. Aoyama is also home to the unconventional Prada store.

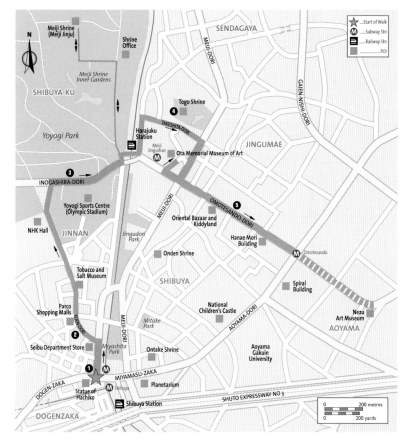

TOKYO ENVIRONS
Atami

Atami has the seen-better-days charm of Blackpool, but with a couple of first-rate attractions: hundreds of hot springs and more geisha than anywhere else in Japan. At weekends, the geisha perform dance shows at the Geigi theatre (*17-13 Chuo-cho*).

1 hour southwest of Tokyo by train.

Boso-hanto (Boso Peninsula)

The Boso-hanto Peninsula in southern Chiba prefecture is surrounded on three sides by water: Tokyo Bay, the Pacific Ocean and the Uraga Channel. Its southern beaches – such as the 55km (34-mile) long Kujukurihama Beach – are sandy and popular among surfers, both local and international.

1½ hours southeast of Tokyo by train.

Tokyo environs

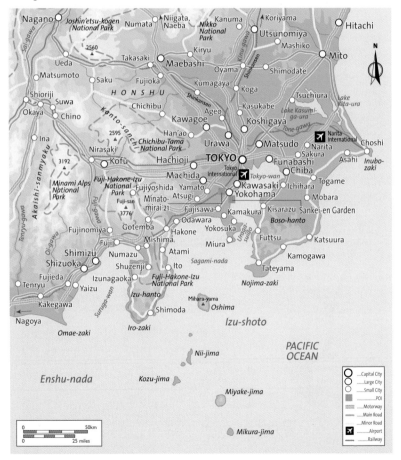

Hot springs

For sheer sybaritic pleasure, there is little to beat the Japanese hot-spring experience. After a hard day's travelling you arrive at your inn, late in the afternoon. You put on the *yukata* (dressing gown) provided and immediately head for the bath. These days there are usually separate baths for men and women, though sometimes the baths are mixed. Always scrub yourself thoroughly outside the tub, rinse off and finally – with a blissful sigh – ease gently into the steaming water. Japanese baths are usually scalding hot, but get in, sit very still and let the heat of the water ease away your tension and tiredness.

The land of Japan is like the lid of a pressure cooker, sitting on a cauldron of volcanic activity. As a result, hot water, laden with healthful minerals, bursts out of the earth all over the country. Different waters are said to be good for different ailments. The water at Atami (*see opposite*) contains calcium sulphate and is good for the nerves and skin, while the waters at Beppu (*see pp136–7*) contain a pot-pourri of minerals that will heal a multitude of ailments – and give you beautiful skin to boot.

Today there are more than 20,000 *onsen* (thermal spas). Besides simple hot tubs, you can bathe in an outdoor pool (*rotenburo*), with the stars twinkling overhead, or sit in a hot waterfall or in the mouth of a cave while the moon rises over the ocean, or be buried up to your neck in mineral-rich hot sand. Most baths are operated by inns, but you don't need to stay there to enjoy a soak. Day tickets, and sometimes private rentals, are offered at most *onsen*.

Taking the waters has always been one of Japan's great pleasures: Beppu's famous hot springs

Fuji-san (Mount Fuji)

See pp56–7.
2½ hours west of Tokyo by bus; or train to Lake Kawaguchi, then bus.

Hakone

On holiday weekends, Tokyoites flock to Hakone for superlative hot springs and a close-up look at Mount Fuji (*see also pp60–61*).
1½ hours southwest of Tokyo by train.

Kamakura

The ancient city of Kamakura has temples, shrines, beautiful gardens, hills good for hiking and even a beach. It is one of Tokyo's most popular seaside resorts, though in summer the beach is barely visible beneath all the people.

Kamakura's heyday lasted from 1180 to 1333. The first shogun, Minamoto Yoritomo, made it his capital and furnished it with spectacular temples and streets lined with cherry trees. Then after bitter fighting, it was defeated by Emperor Go-Daigo. Power reverted to Kyoto, and Kamakura became a charming getaway that now oozes nostalgia.

Hase-dera (Hase Temple)

The grounds of this ancient temple are blanketed with images of Jizo, the bodhisattva (divine being) responsible for children. Mothers who have miscarried or had abortions clothe the small statues with bibs. But the glory of the temple is its towering 9m (30ft) camphor-wood *juichi-men* (11-faced) Kannon, deity of mercy. Legend has it that it was carved in the Nara area, then cast into the sea to find its divinely appointed place. It drifted ashore at Kamakura in 736.
5-minute walk from Hase station.
Open: Mar–Sept daily 8am–5pm (till 4.30pm in winter). Admission charge.

Kotokuin Daibutsu (Great Buddha)

The Great Buddha is the symbol of Kamakura. The seated figure is 11.4m (37ft) tall – as big as a small house – and towers above the surrounding trees. Cast in bronze in 1252, the Buddha sits, his eyes cast down in meditation, emanating peace and serenity. The temple which once housed the image was washed away by a tidal wave in 1495, and ever since, the Buddha has sat out in the open.
10-minute walk from Hase station.
Open: daily 7am–6pm (till 5.30pm in winter). Admission charge.

Tsurugaoka Hachiman-gu (Hachiman Shrine)

The shrine to Hachiman, god of war, is the heart of Kamakura. Leave the station and you come almost immediately to a broad avenue crossed by huge *torii* (gates). This is Wakamiya Oji (Avenue of the Young Prince), which leads from the beach all the way to Hachiman Shrine.

Founded in 1063, the shrine was moved to its present position on Tsurugaoka (Crane Hill) by Shogun Minamoto Yoritomo in 1191. As you approach it, you come to Drum Bridge, as steep as the side of a drum, which only the shogun was allowed to cross. The shrine itself, a splendid vermilion structure, is at the top of a long flight of steps; if you look back you see the sea behind you.

Hachiman is always bustling with people. Not to be missed is the archery contest on 16 September, when mounted archers in medieval costume, galloping at full pelt, send arrows winging to hit three small targets.
10-minute walk from Kamakura station. Always open. Free admission.

Zeniarai Benten

Enclosed within a natural cavern, surrounded by moss and dangling tree roots, this atmospheric old shrine is full of ponds, small shrines, altars, fortune-tellers and incense smoke. It is said that if you wash your money here, it will double in value: put your cash in the wicker baskets, then dry the notes in the incense smoke.
25-minute walk west of Kamakura station. Always open. Free admission.

Kamakura is 1 hour south of Tokyo by train (see also pp62–3).

Kawagoe

This small castle town retains something of the flavour of old Edo (pre-modern Tokyo). After a disastrous fire in 1893, many fireproof storehouses and shops were built with thick walls of clay and plaster, tiny shuttered windows and steep tiled roofs. Several of these handsome black buildings line the main shopping street. Be sure not to miss **Kita-en Temple**, the birthplace of Shogun Tokugawa Ieyasu.
55 minutes northwest of Tokyo by train. Kita-en Temple. 10-minute walk from Hon-Kawagoe station. Open: Apr–Nov daily 9am–4.30pm (till 4pm in winter). Admission charge.

Kamakura's spectacular Great Buddha keeps watch over the city

Miura

Beyond Kamakura is the Miura Peninsula, one of the nearest areas of countryside to Tokyo. Off the main roads there is good walking, beaches,

Naeba is famous for its powder on- and off-piste

old temples and picturesque fishing villages. Miura is particularly associated with the British navigator Will Adams, whose life inspired the novel and film *Shogun*. Blown off-course, Adams dropped anchor in Japan in 1600. He struck up a friendship with the shogun Tokugawa Ieyasu and taught the Japanese the art of shipbuilding.
1½ hours south of Tokyo by rail and road.

Mount Naeba

Only two hours from Tokyo, Naeba is the perfect spot for communing with nature all year round. Mount Naeba peaks at 2,145m (7,037ft) above sea level and this peaceful mountain region boasts green hiking trails in the spring and canyoning in the summer. In the autumn, there are red leaves and hot springs in the area, such as Kaikake *onsen* and Akayu *onsen*, and in the winter there are powder-filled ski slopes.

To the west of Mount Naeba is Akiyama-go, which is said to be an ancient hideout for soldiers who lost battles with Genji, the Kamakura shogunate.
1 hour 10 minutes north from Tokyo station to Echigo-yuzawa by train; 50 minutes from Echigo-yuzawa to Naeba Prince Hotel by bus.

Oshima Island

Scattered south of Tokyo are seven islands, an extension of the Fuji-Hakone volcanic chain. At the centre of the largest, Oshima, is **Mount Mihara**

(Mihara-yama), which erupted spectacularly in 1986 for several months. Today it is placid and Oshima has regained its status as Tokyo's nearest tropical paradise. There is a wonderful outdoor hot spring on Mount Mihara, in a cave overhung with vines and creepers, and the mountaintop affords fine views of Mount Fuji and the seven islands. Oshima is known as Camellia Island for its beautiful camellia bushes, which produce an oil used to gloss sumo wrestlers' hair.

Accessible by plane and ferry (by air 50 minutes from Tokyo Haneda Airport).

Yokohama

Yokohama is a lively city famous for its international flavour. The arrival of the first Western ships 150 years ago turned it into the country's most important port. Westerners were encouraged to settle here, at a safe distance from Tokyo, and there is still a large Western community along with a thriving cricket club. Yokohama is now Japan's second-largest city and a vital commercial and industrial hub.

The city itself is very pleasant. It has the largest **Chinatown** in Japan, and people come here to imbibe the exotic atmosphere and dine on the country's best Chinese food.

On the southeast edge of the city is **Sankei-en Garden**, laid out by Tomitaro Hara, a silk magnate, in 1906. Scattered around the beautifully landscaped grounds are villas, tea pavilions, farmhouses and a 500-year-old pagoda that were brought here from all over Japan.

Yokohama's profile is changing rapidly. There is a splendid new Bay Bridge across the harbour, glittering at night, which you can admire from the soaring skyscrapers that make up the futuristic Minato-mirai 21 development.

30 minutes south of Tokyo by train; also accessible by plane, ship and road. Chinatown. At Ishikawa-cho station. Sankei-en Garden. 10-minute walk from Yamate station. Outer garden open: daily 9am–4.30pm. Inner garden open: daily 9am–4pm. Admission charge to each.

Minato-mirai 21

Just north of Sakuragi-cho station, there are several attractions worth visiting here. The **Landmark Tower**, the tallest building in Japan, has an observatory on the 69th floor (the Landmark Tower Sky Garden) offering a unique view across Yokohama. Close by are the **Yokohama Maritime Museum**, **Cosmo World** amusement park and two large shopping/dining complexes: **Yokohama World Porters** and **Queens Square Yokohama**. Stop by the Tourist Information Centre outside the northern exit of Sakuragi-cho station for a free copy of the *Yokohama City Guide*.

TIC. Open: daily 9am–6pm. Maritime Museum. Tel: 04 5221 0280. Open: Tue–Sun 10am–5pm. Admission charge.

Mount Fuji

Mount Fuji, or Fuji-san, is probably the most recognisable symbol of Japan to foreigners, and a symbol of culture for the Japanese.

Mount Fuji is a dormant volcano, and at a height of 3,776m (12,388ft) is Japan's highest mountain, which, on a clear day, can be seen from Tokyo and Yokohama. The apex is broken by a cone-shaped crater 610m (2,000ft) in diameter. Although the symmetry of the mountain, forming a cone, is often remarked on, the mountain is actually more complicated. The cone called Mount Fuji is actually the result of four phases of volcanic activity: Sen-komitake, Komitake Fuji, Older Fuji and Younger Fuji. If you look closely at the silhouette, you can see irregularities that are a result of this overlap (a slight bump on the

Mount Fuji and the bullet train are two of Japan's most recognisable symbols

northern slope at about 2,300m (7,546ft) is part of the summit crater of Komitake, the oldest of the three volcanoes).

Although the mountain is now considered dormant, it has a long history of eruptions. The most recent (called the Hoei eruption) occurred on 24 November 1707, lasted for two months and is said to have been Mount Fuji's most violent.

During the climbing season, from July to August, roughly 400,000 people make the long trek up the mountain, most commonly timed to see the sun rise from the summit. Mount Fuji also has a religious significance and annually around 10,000 pilgrims make their way to the summit.

Given the natural beauty of Mount Fuji, it's not surprising that it has played a central role in Japanese culture. The mountain has inspired many of Japan's most famous artists and poets and featured in many folk stories and myths.

Arguably the most famous artist inspired by the mountain is Hokusai, who immortalised it in his *36 Views of Mount Fuji*. Katsushika Hokusai (1760–1849) was a painter and wood engraver who was born in Edo (now Tokyo). He is considered to be one of the most outstanding artists of the *ukiyo-e* school of printmaking. Between the mid-1790s and early 1800s he created a huge number of illustrations and colour prints (some estimates are as high as 20,000), which drew their influence from Japanese traditions and legends. He is best known for his landscapes, and by far his most famous work is his 36-picture set *Views of Mount Fuji*, which he produced in 1827, to which he added ten further views over the following decade.

The kanji (Chinese-derived written script) used to write the name of Mount Fuji has changed over time and has had various meanings such as 'the mountain of warriors' or 'without equal', and in the language of the indigenous Ainu (*see pp72–3*) 'Funchi' means 'fire god' or 'volcano'.

Fuji is notoriously shy and very often hidden behind a veil of cloud, but on a fine day you can see it from Tokyo. There are good views from the bullet train, from Hakone and from the lakes at its base.

The Fuji Five Lakes region is a popular resort area for Tokyoites. Lake Yamanaka is a rich man's playground, with golf courses, watersports and villas. Kawaguchi is the most accessible, Lake Sai is famous for its mysterious lava caves, and Lake Motosu is the deepest. The prettiest is Lake Shoji, surrounded by wooded hills on three sides, with a beautiful view of Fuji soaring above the trees.

Walk: Climbing Mount Fuji

Everyone wants to climb Fuji once – though, as the Japanese proverb goes, only a fool would climb it twice. The official climbing season is July and August. During this period, buses run straight from Tokyo to the fifth station and the mountain huts along the path are open.

Fuji is a real mountain. Be prepared for cold and sudden changes in weather; even at the height of summer it is freezing cold and very windy at the top. It is also high enough, at 3,776m (12,388ft), to produce mild altitude sickness. You will need a sweater, rainwear, hat and gloves, hiking boots, a torch and a walking stick.

Allow 2 days and 1 night. Just climbing Mount Fuji from the fifth station (call Fuji Kyuko, tel: 05 5522 7112) is possible as a day trip from Tokyo, if you leave early enough. Check with Tokyo TIC for seasonal transport link times.

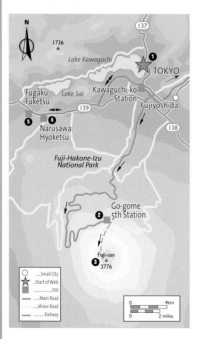

1 Kawaguchi-ko (Lake Kawaguchi)

On a fine day you can see Fuji, very close, gloriously reflected in the lake.
Buses leave hourly for the 50-minute journey to the fifth station.

2 Go-gome (Fifth Station)

Many people go to the Kawaguchi-ko fifth station for a day trip. From here, halfway up Fuji, you can stroll along a broad, level path with stunning views across the surrounding country.
Expect to take 5 hours to reach the summit from Kawaguchi-ko fifth station. The climbing path is well marked.

3 The summit

The path starts off steep and gets ever steeper. From the sixth station you are above the tree line, walking on dusty volcanic gravel. The climb from the seventh to the ninth stations is the hardest. At each station there are a *torii* and a shrine, and also huts where you can buy a bowl of noodles – for the Japanese, this is a pilgrimage as well as a hike. If you want to see the sunrise, rest at the seventh or eighth stations and finish the climb just before dawn.

Arriving at the summit is a truly exhilarating experience. There is a *torii* across the path and a shrine at the top, where a Shinto priest conducts a dawn ceremony. There are also a souvenir shop, a post office, some vending machines and noodle shops. With luck the sunrise will be a breathtakingly beautiful, pale lemon spreading across the sky with clouds rolling below you. As the sun rises, watch for the huge shadow of Fuji spread across the clouds. It takes an hour to walk around the crater (the highest point is marked by the weather station on the far side).
Return the way you came, or take the Sunabashiri route, sliding on volcanic gravel, back to the fifth station in 2½– 3 hours. From here return to Tokyo; or take a bus to Narusawa cave, via Lake Kawaguchi.

4 Narusawa Hyoketsu (Narusawa Ice Cave)

Near Fuji there are two caves formed by pockets of gas trapped in the lava

A landscape worthy of a watercolour rendering

during an eruption thousands of years ago. Narusawa Ice Cave is icy cold, even at the height of summer.
Take the hiking trail through the woods to Fugaku Wind Cave.

5 Fugaku Fuketsu (Fugaku Wind Cave)

Fugaku Wind Cave is a series of caverns, with towering stalagmites.
From here take a bus back to Lake Kawaguchi and thence to Tokyo.

The **Mount Fuji English Climbing Info** telephone/fax service is supplied free of charge by Fuji Yoshida Tourist Information Office (*tel: 05 5522 7000*).

Tour: Hakone

This circuit of the lovely Hakone region, by mountain railway, funicular railway, cable car and boat, can be done as a day trip from Tokyo; or stop over at a hot-spring inn. On a fine day there are wonderful views of Fuji.

At the Odakyu line station in Shinjuku, buy a 'free pass' which gives you unlimited travel in Hakone on most transport for two or three days. If you are using a JR train pass, buy one at Odawara station. Take the train to Odawara.

1 Odawara

Odawara was once an important castle town. The present castle is a 1960 reconstruction of the 1416 original.
At Odawara station, board the Hakone-Tozan mountain railway, which toils slowly up the wooded hillside. Alight at Miyanoshita. Turn left out of the station and stroll up the hill through the village.

2 Miyanoshita

Miyanoshita is a famous Japanese spa and home to the glorious old Fujiya Hotel. Built in 1878, the Fujiya trades heavily on having hosted both Charlie Chaplin and John Lennon.
Take the Hakone-Tozan railway on to Chokoku-no-mori.

3 Chokoku-no-mori (Hakone Open-air Sculpture Museum)

Spread across the hillside are modern sculptures by both Western and Japanese artists, including one of the world's largest collections of works by British sculptor Henry Moore. There is

also a museum devoted to the ceramics of Pablo Picasso.
3-min walk from Chokoku-no-mori station. Tel: 0460 82 1161. Open: daily 9am–5pm. Admission charge.
Take the Hakone-Tozan railway on to the terminus, Gora. Change there for the funicular railway which takes you to Sounzan station. From there take the Hakone Ropeway cable car.

4 Owakudani

The cable car swings high above a spectacular volcanic landscape, with glorious views of Fuji. Halfway across, alight at Owakudani ('Great Boiling Valley'), from where you can stroll between boiling mud pools and vents of sulphurous steam and buy an egg boiled in spring water.
Take the cable car on to the terminus, Togendai.

5 Lake Ashi

At Togendai, you can sail across Lake Ashi, the heart of Hakone, by mock

Spanish galleon or by standard – and more frequent – ferry. On fine days Mount Fuji soars above this lovely lake, perfectly mirrored in its waters. There are hotels, watersports and fine hiking here. To your left, as you near the town of Hakone, watch for the red *torii* of Hakone Shrine, standing in the water. *Alight at the dock at Hakone-machi (Hakone town) and walk left from the port through the village to Hakone Checkpoint.*

6 Hakone Sekisho (Checkpoint)

In the days of the shoguns, all travellers on the main road between Edo (old Tokyo) and Kyoto had to stop at this police checkpoint, where they were thoroughly searched. The museum contains weapons and photographs of criminals' severed heads, on poles. *Hakone Sekisho museum. Open: Mar–Nov daily 9am–5pm (till 4.30pm in winter). Admission charge.*

Take the footpath lined with cedars along the edge of the lake to Hakone Shrine, just beyond Moto-Hakone village. There are also buses.

7 Hakone Shrine

This beautiful old shrine, founded in 757, stands in a grove of ancient cryptomeria trees. From here, go down the steps to the lakeside, where the large red *torii* stands in the water.

From Moto-Hakone take a bus back to Odawara, from where there are frequent trains back to Tokyo.

Tour: Hakone

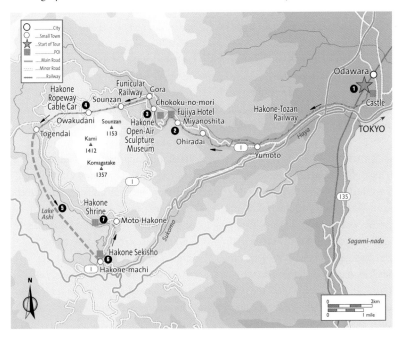

Walk: Kita-Kamakura and Kamakura

This walk takes you from the serene Zen temples of Kita-Kamakura (North Kamakura), along a trail through the hills, to Kamakura's celebrated Hachiman Shrine.

Allow 4 hours.

Kita-Kamakura is 55 minutes south of Tokyo by train. Engakuji is just outside the station.

1 Engakuji

Many laypeople come to this famous Zen temple, founded in 1282, to learn Zen meditation. The path to the left of the main hall leads via the relic hall and a thatched sub-temple, where you can have green tea, to an attractive garden. The path to the right leads to the temple's Great Bell, cast in 1301.
Open: Apr–Oct daily 8am–5pm (till 4pm in winter). Admission charge.
Return to the road and follow the tracks to a level crossing. Turn left along the main road to the huge gate of Kenchoji.

2 Kenchoji

This is the oldest Zen temple in Japan. Pass the Great Gate and the atmospheric old Buddha Hall, which houses a statue of Jizo, the bodhisattva who protects children. Don't miss the fine Zen garden behind the Dragon Hall, with a pond shaped like the character for 'heart'. Follow the path on and up to a *torii* and two stone lions, marking the entrance to Hansobo.

Climb up to this strange little shrine, past images of 'mountain goblins' – winged and beaked mountain priests.
Tel: 0467 22 0981. Open: daily 8.30am–4.30pm. Admission charge.
Take the stone steps up on to the hill. There is a clear hiking trail along the ridge, through woods and bamboo groves. After 30 minutes, you come to a large signpost where two paths cross. Take the right-hand path down to a road. Kakuonji is 250m (273yd) up the road to your right.

3 Kakuonji

Kakuonji is a peaceful retreat, tucked away at the end of a long valley. If you arrive on the hour on a fine day (except in August), one of the monks will show you the temple's Buddha images and the Black Jizo, said to rescue sinners from hell.
Open: daily for tours at 10am, 11am, 1pm, 2pm & 3pm, except on rainy days. Closed: Aug & 20 Dec–7 Jan. Admission charge.

Go down the road to Kamakura Shrine (1869). Follow the road to your right to another road, signposted in English 'Egara Tenjin Shrine'. This small backstreet leads to Hachiman Shrine.

4 Tsurugaoka Hachiman-gu (Hachiman Shrine)

Along the way, you can drop in to Egara Tenjin Shrine, dedicated to the god of scholarship. You also pass the tomb of the first shogun, Minamoto Yoritomo. At a T-junction, turn left, then right,

and you will find the avenue used for horseback archery every 16 September. After exploring Hachiman-gu (*see pp52–3*), you can stroll down the broad avenue which leads from the front of the shrine, built by Shogun Minamoto Yoritomo in 1182. At cherry blossom time this is particularly beautiful. Or turn right from the shrine entrance, then left down Komachi-dori (Komachi Street), full of restaurants, teahouses and souvenir shops.

You will end up at Kamakura station.

Walk: Kita-Kamakura and Kamakura

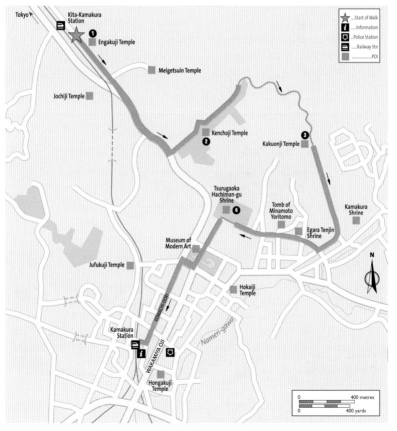

Ukiyo-e and *irezumi*

Ukiyo-e is a genre of Japanese woodblock print that blossomed in the height of the Edo era in the late 17th century. This was a time when an impetuous youth culture arose, and Edo (Tokyo), Kyoto and Osaka were filled with geisha, teahouses, brothels and kabuki theatres. *Ukiyo-e* captured images of the *ukiyo*, or the 'floating world': a world full of transitory pleasure and free from care.

The art form first became popular with Hishikawa Mornobu's monochrome prints in 1670. Katsushika Hokusai (*see p57*) is another famous *ukiyo-e* artist, whose *36 Views of Mount Fuji* – and in particular *The Great Wave off Kanagawa* – are still iconic.

The transition from paper to skin came as *ukiyo-e* artists swapped their woodcarving blades for sharp needles bundled into the end of a bamboo rod. Using charcoal ink inserted under the skin, they carved pictures of daily life, landscape,

Hokusai's famous *36 Views of Mount Fuji: The Great Wave off Kanagawa*

The intricate artwork that is *irezumi*

kabuki, onto a live canvas, covering vast areas of their subjects' bodies. This process is known as *tebori*. The *tebori* craftsmen would often tattoo full bodysuits for their clients: covering the tops of the legs, the torso and the arms. The inspiration for the bodysuit came from the samurai *jimbaori*, or warrior's campaign coat. The artists turned to Japanese and Chinese myths and folklore for inspiration for their tattoos: depicting anything from animals and flowers to gods and *namakubi*, or beheadings.

Many of these craftsmen never went back to woodcarving, becoming professional tattooists for life, passing on their skills to an apprentice (often the artist's son) over the course of years and years of rigorous training. The art of *irezumi* – or the insertion of ink under the skin – has always been an underground one, however, and it remains the same today. Anyone with tattoos is banned from entering *onsen* as well as certain gyms, due to a long-term association with the yakuza, or Japanese mafia.

Despite its negative connotations, there are some superb *irezumi* artists in Japan, including Hoshinoya III, who followed the traditional apprenticeship route.

The north

The north is a region of magnificent unspoilt scenery, with primeval landscapes created by volcanic eruptions and sweeping vistas of lakes, mountains and forests. Visitors come here to enjoy nature rather than the works of man: there are few temples, castles or monuments to traditional Japanese culture.

This is traditionally the poorest, most underprivileged part of the country. Both Tohoku – the northern part of Honshu – and Hokkaido were originally the home of Japan's earliest settlers, who were gradually driven north by later arrivals. Colonisation of Hokkaido began in the 1800s, and here you can still see remnants of the culture of the island's original inhabitants, the Ainu (*see pp72–3*).

The region is largely agricultural. Country life goes on much as it did hundreds of years ago, and there is much of old Japan here, although Hokkaido, especially the Hakodate area, also has a slight European feel to it due to the influence of nearby Russia. Recently, it has also become a prime holiday area. In winter people come to ski, in summer to walk or play golf.

The greatest walker of all was the 17th-century poet Matsuo Basho (*see box on p100*), who roamed the Tohoku region 300 years ago and wrote both groundbreaking haikus and a travel diary, *The Narrow Road to the Deep North*. Throughout the north are places he immortalised in his exquisite poems.

Hokkaido prefecture:
www.pref.hokkaido.lg.jp.
Miyagi prefecture:
www.pref.miyagi.jp.
Tohoku:
www.northern-tohoku.gr.jp

THE *YAMABUSHI*

The wandering ascetic priests called *yamabushi* are the guardians of the sacred mountains. They could be found all over Japan, clad in their distinctive garb of black pillbox hat, checked blouse and deerskin leggings, and carrying a huge conch shell which they blew like a horn. They practised Shugendo, a form of Tantric Buddhism, and often performed the role of sorcerers and exorcists.

Nowadays many apparent *yamabushi* turn out to be farmers or businessmen taking a few days off, though you can still find full-time *yamabushi* leading pilgrims across the three sacred mountains.

Hokkaido, awash with sunflowers

Akan National Park

In a primeval forest, **Lake Akan** is dotted with curious balls of green algae known as *marimo*, some of which are hundreds of years old. Nearby, **Lake Kussharo** is Japan's Loch Ness, said to be home to a monster nicknamed Kusshi. The scenery is breathtaking (*see also p146*).

Hokkaido. Approach by bus or rented car from Bihoro, 5 hours by train east of Sapporo.

Daisetsuzan National Park

Daisetsuzan's beauties lie at two levels. Below, accessible by car, is **Sounkyo Gorge** with its ravines and vertiginous cliff faces, one of Hokkaido's most famous sights. Above, the domain of hikers and skiers, are the spectacular peaks, a landscape of dark, cinder-sloped volcanic cones and craters, where icy winds blow even at the height of summer and steam gushes from the ground. There is an Ainu museum in the city of **Asahikawa**, on the far side of the park, where you can see Ainu dances (*see also pp146–7*).

Hokkaido. Approach from Asahikawa or Kamikawa, 1½–2 hours northeast of Sapporo by train, then by bus or rented car.

Dewa Sanzan (Three Mountains of Dewa)

The three mountains of Dewa (the old name for northeast Tohoku) are among the most sacred in Japan, strewn with temples and small stone shrines. Japanese come from all over the country on pilgrimage, and even the least religious cannot fail to feel the power of the place. Holiest is **Mount Yudono**, home of a deity who resides in a hot spring. Nearby are two temples with the remains of *yamabushi* (*see box opposite*) who literally mummified themselves in order to become Buddhas before their deaths (*see also p148*).

Tohoku. 1½ hours by bus northwest of Yamagata; accessible by plane or train (2 hours) from Tokyo.

Hakodate

For centuries the Japanese toehold on Hokkaido was the port city of Hakodate, at its southernmost tip. Since 1740 Russia had used Hakodate as a landing base. When the West forced Japan to open to trade in 1854, Hakodate was one of the first treaty ports, and the city still retains its historic flavour.

Goryaku Fort, with its five-pointed star-shaped grounds, is Japan's first Western-style fort. This is where the army of the Tokugawa shogunate made its last stand against the army of the Emperor Meiji. Take the cable car up **Mount Hakodate** for a spectacular night view over the city; stroll the streets of the old town, Motomachi, full of well-preserved Meiji-period buildings; or take a cruise across the bay.

Hokkaido. 4 hours south of Sapporo by train; also accessible by plane.

Hiraizumi

In his *Travels,* the 15th-century Venetian, Marco Polo, wrote of a country called 'Zipangu', where the palaces were of solid gold. The city he was describing was Hiraizumi. For a hundred years, between 1089 and 1189, Hiraizumi was the heart of a vibrant culture, based on gold mining. The town still has several reminders of its glory years.

One small temple completely covered in gold leaf still remains – the **Konjikido** (Golden Hall), part of **Chusonji**. The Golden Hall houses

YOSHITSUNE

The epic *Tale of the Heike* and numerous kabuki and Noh dramas celebrate the exploits of Japan's great medieval hero, Minamoto-no Yoshitsune. When Yoshitsune was born in 1159, two warrior clans – the Taira and Minamoto – were battling to rule Japan. He led the Minamoto to victory, but his elder brother, Shogun Yoritomo, was jealous of his success and demanded his head. Accompanied by a few faithful retainers, Yoshitsune fled north and in 1189 took refuge in the independent kingdom of Hiraizumi. His trust was misplaced. The ruler, the treacherous Yasuhira, surrounded Yoshitsune's castle, where the hero's retainers defended him just long enough for him to commit honourable suicide. Yasuhira's treachery did not pay off. The shogun attacked the northern kingdom and the great civilisation of Hiraizumi came to an end.

a statue of Amida, Buddha of the Western Paradise, surrounded by attendants. Buried beneath the three altars are the three Fujiwara lords who ruled Hiraizumi during its heyday. The poet Basho visited in 1689 and wrote one of his most famous haiku:

> '*Summer grasses*
> *– the aftermath*
> *of ancient warriors'*
> *dreams!*'

Takadachi Gikeido is a temple housing a wooden statue of just one such warrior: Minamoto-no Yoshitsune. Also worth visiting is **Motsuji**, a temple that was once a pleasure garden of princes and nobles, who whiled away their days composing verses while paddling languidly in boats and sipping sake.

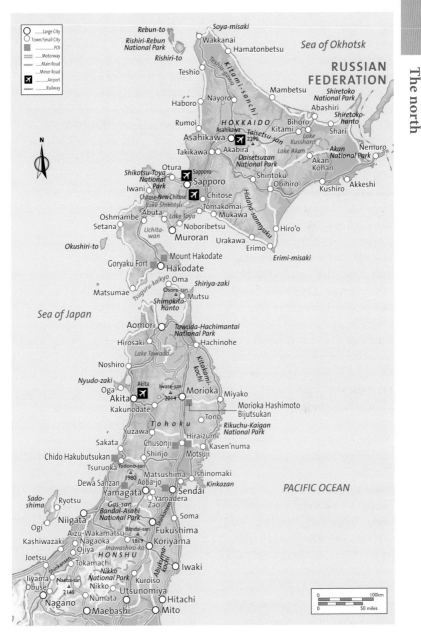

Tohoku. About 3 hours north of Tokyo by train.
Chusonji. 20-minute walk from station. Open: Apr–Oct daily 8am–5pm; 8.30am–4.30pm in winter. Admission charge.
Motsuji. 10-minute walk from station. Open: Apr–Oct daily 8.30am–5pm (till 4.30pm in winter). Admission charge.

Hirosaki

This charming northern city preserves much of the flavour of the past. It was formerly the capital of the Tsugaru clan, who ruled over the rugged northernmost province of Honshu. It has two sights well worth stopping for, both oases of tranquillity. The 17th-century temple, **Choshoji**, with its massive triple-storey front gate, is flanked by an avenue of 33 temples, lined with pine trees. **Hirosaki Castle**, one of the few genuinely old castles remaining in Japan, stands on a bluff above the town, in a pleasant park and surrounded by three moats covered in water lilies.

Tohoku. About 4 hours by road or rail northwest of Morioka.

Kakunodate

Kakunodate is famous for its streets of lovely old samurai houses, lined with dark wooden fences overhung with luxuriant weeping cherry trees. The town was carefully planned at the beginning of the Tokugawa shogunate era, around 1620, with two completely separate areas – one for merchants, one for samurai – divided by an open plaza which acted as a firebreak. The merchant quarter has grown into a modern commercial centre, but much of the samurai district is lovingly preserved. Some of the poorer samurai made a living by making cups, vases and tea ceremony caddies covered in polished cherry bark; many shops in the area specialise in this attractive handicraft.

Tohoku. 45 minutes west of Morioka by train. Samurai houses. Open: Apr–Nov daily 9am–5pm (till 4.30pm in winter). Admission charge for some; others free.

Matsushima

When the poet Basho visited Matsushima Bay in 1689, he was so overcome by its beauty that he could not write a single word. Matsushima – the name means 'pine islands' – is still exquisitely beautiful, with tiny craggy islets crowned with gnarled pines, set in a jewel-blue sea. You can stroll the shoreline, studded with islands and temples, including the ancient Zen temple of Zuiganji, or take a boat around the outlying islands. You will, however, share your enjoyment with thousands of others. Matsushima is one of the three most celebrated views in Japan, a popular holiday and honeymoon spot, full of people and hotels. For those in search of peace and quiet, the tranquil paddy fields and hills of nearby Oku Matsushima and the island of Kinkazan, home to deer and monkeys, are a better bet.

Tohoku. 35 minutes north of Sendai by train.

Morioka

Once the castle town of the lords of Nambu, Morioka is a large, pleasant city, surrounded by densely forested hills. Nothing remains of the castle except the moat and some ruinous walls, but across the river is an attractive artisans' area with many old shops, housing dyers, metalworkers and bakers of *sembei* (rice crackers).

On Mount Iwate, with a fine view across the city, is an eccentric museum created by a local 19th-century artist, Yaoji Hashimoto. It rambles through several ancient and beautifully renovated farmhouses, and includes fine examples of local ironware, pottery and handicrafts as well as the artist's own paintings.

Tohoku. 2½–3½ hours north of Tokyo by train.

Morioka Hashimoto Bijutsukan (Morioka Hashimoto Museum of Art).

30 minutes by bus from station.

Tel: 019 652 5002.

Open: daily 10am–5pm.

Admission charge.

Views of Mount Iwate from the Kitakami River, Morioka

The north

The Ainu

Dotted around the lakesides and plains of Hokkaido are totem poles, small houses with thatched roofs and souvenir stalls selling wooden carvings, vestiges of a near-vanished culture.

Hokkaido and northeastern Honshu were formerly the domain of a variety of tribes known as the Ainu. Racially they are distinct from the Japanese, with lighter skin, a heavier brow ridge and deep-set eyes, sometimes grey or blue. The men are distinguished

Intricate embroidery on a traditional Ainu costume

by their luxuriant head hair, beards and moustaches.

The Ainu once lived by hunting, fishing and gathering plants. They made bows and arrows, carved canoes from tree trunks, and wore robes of elm-bark or cotton, appliquéd with distinctive geometric whorls. When the women married they tattooed around their mouths.

They had a rich oral culture, epic poems passed from generation to generation. They worshipped the spirits of animals and plants, especially the bear, owl and sea turtle. Once a year they performed the Iomante ceremony, a form of fertility festival in which a bear was sacrificed and its spirit sent heavenward.

For centuries the Ainu were driven further and further north, and after the Japanese colonised Hokkaido in 1868 they became second-class citizens. Today, after a century of intermarriage, there are only 25,000 full-blooded Ainu left, plus another 25,000 who are part-Japanese. The Ainu language has nearly died out with few young people able to speak it, but in recent years the younger Ainu have begun to take a pride in their ancestral heritage. There is a growing Ainu movement and in August 1994 a leading Ainu activist won a seat in the Upper House of the Japanese Diet.

Visitors can get a glimpse of this disappearing Ainu world in a few museums and rather sad Ainu villages, where customs and handicrafts are preserved and impoverished Ainu elders conduct their ancient ceremonies, rituals and dances.

A reconstruction of an Ainu dwelling in Nibutani, Hokkaido

Nikko

No emperor ever had a monument as overwhelmingly lavish as the shogun's tomb at Nikko. After Tokugawa Ieyasu's death, his grandson Iemitsu planned a mausoleum that would demonstrate the shogunate's incredible wealth and power. To finance it, he took 'donations' from the daimyo, thus ensuring that none would ever be able to finance a rebellion. The Toshogu Shrine took two years to complete, starting in 1634. An army of 15,000 artisans worked on it; 38 tonnes (37 tons) of red lacquer and 2.5 million sheets of gold leaf coated its walls.

The ornate buildings are in a spectacular mountain setting, surrounded by ancient cryptomeria forests. Nearby are Lake Chuzenji, which on a clear day reflects the volcanic cone of Mount Nantai in its waters, and the mighty Kegon Falls.

Nikko is one of Japan's most popular destinations. Try to visit early or late to avoid the crowds. Before entering the shrines, buy a strip of tickets allowing entry into the four main sights (paying separately for each costs far more).

Rinnoji

Rinnoji dates from AD 766; the present magnificent buildings were rebuilt as part of Iemitsu's grand plan. The main hall houses three massive gilt Buddhist images.

Shinkyo

This beautiful old bridge of faded red and gold marks the approach to the

---

TOKUGAWA IEYASU (1543–1616)

In the mid-16th century, Japan was racked by civil war as one warlord after another strove to expand his domains and take over the country. Warlord Tokugawa Ieyasu defeated the last of his enemies in 1600, became shogun and instituted the system that was to keep the country at peace and under the control of the Tokugawa family for the next 250 years. After his death, he was interred at Nikko; the Toshogu Shrine was later built as his mausoleum.

---

shrines. In the past only shoguns and Imperial envoys could cross.

Taiyuin-byo

The last complex you come to, set against the mountain, is the mausoleum of Tokugawa Iemitsu. In structure it is a smaller version of the Toshogu Shrine, but different in style, less ornate, more unified and sophisticated. Brilliantly painted green and red deities stand against a background of peonies. Look for the Kokamon beside the main shrine, said to resemble the gate of the legendary Dragon King's palace under the sea.

Toshogu Shrine

The Toshogu Shrine is a far cry from the Zen restraint which Westerners associate with Japanese aesthetics. Every possible surface is covered in ornamentation: animals, sages, gods and birds peep from every frieze and cornice. The buildings are arranged on a series of levels, and gates – each more splendid than the last – lead deep into the heart of the shrine.

In the first enclosure, look for the relief of two elephants, carved by an artist who had clearly never seen one, and the three wise monkeys, an emblem of Nikko.

The most dazzling and famous structure is the Yomeimon, nicknamed the Twilight Gate because you could spend all day from dawn to dusk looking at it. One of the pillars is carved upside down, to stop the gods being jealous of such perfection. Lower-ranking samurai could not pass this gate. Beyond is the main shrine, dedicated to Ieyasu, and – at the top of 207 steps – the small tomb containing his ashes.

Nikko Tourist Information Centre.
Tel: 0288 54 2496.
Nikko shrines and temples. Open:
Apr–Oct daily 8am–5pm (till 4pm in winter). Admission charge (you can buy tickets for each attraction individually, but it is cheaper to buy a combined ticket which covers all the main sites, except the Nemuri-Neki, meaning Sleeping Cat, in Toshogu).

Nikko is 2 hours north of Tokyo by train. Tourist information office at station.

The unusually ornate Toshogu Shrine

Noboribetsu

The pungent smell of sulphur and steam greets you in Noboribetsu, Hokkaido's most famous spa. For those partial to hot-spring bathing, the Dai-ichi Takimoto-kan has over 40 different sorts of baths. You can visit the Ainu village, or Jigoku-dani (Hell Valley) behind the town, where mud pools boil and sputter and steam jets into the air.
Hokkaido. 1 hour by train south of Sapporo, then 15 minutes by bus to the spa.

Obihiro

Outdoor lovers will enjoy a visit to Obihiro, the main city in the Tokachi region of Hokkaido, where green landscapes roll and grazing cows pasture. There is no shortage of activities here: hot-air ballooning and canoeing from the southwestern side of Lake Shikaribetsu are particularly popular. For those who want to relax, Obihiro is also a jumping-off point for Tokachi *onsen*, where the weather is renowned for smoothing the skin.

Osore-zan (Mount Osore)

Osore-zan, in the far northeast of Honshu, is one of the weirdest places on earth and worth the enormous difficulty of getting there. The time to see this unearthly volcanic landscape is in July, when people come from as far as Tokyo to consult blind mediums in the temple on the edge of the crater lake (*see also pp148–9*).

A PRIEST CALLED NICHIREN

During the 1250s a series of natural disasters decimated Japan. Believing that the gods were abandoning Japan, a priest, Nichiren, prophesied that the disasters would end in a foreign invasion destroying the Kamaura shogunate unless his sect was made the official religion of Japan. The shogun ordered Nichiren to be executed for inciting rebellion, but as the executioner raised his sword it was split in two by lightning. The shogun then exiled Nichiren to Sado. In 1274 Nichiren's prophesy was fulfilled when Kublai Khan invaded Japan. The shogun asked for Nichiren's help, and a kamikaze (divine wind) occurred, resulting in the defeat of the Mongol horde. These events were repeated in 1281, and Nichiren, credited with saving Japan twice, was pardoned. His sect, Nichiren-shu, is still active today.

Tohoku. 35 minutes by infrequent bus from Mutsu; 2 hours by train north of Aomori. Aomori is accessible by plane; 5 hours north of Tokyo by train.

Sado-shima (Sado Island)

Peaceful, unspoilt Sado, off Honshu's northwest coast, is a microcosm of Japan, with four distinct seasons, a wealth of history and lush green hills and terraced paddy fields. The fifth largest of Japan's islands, Sado was traditionally a place of exile for revolutionaries. After 1601, when gold was found at Aikawa in the remote northwest, criminals were sent to toil in the mines. Ferries arrive at Ryotsu, the main port, and from there you can explore the island by bus or rented car. You can tour the mines, visit weatherbeaten little fishing villages or camp or hike in summer.

Sado is famous for its Noh theatre, due in part to Zeami, a Japanese Shakespeare who was exiled here in the early 1440s. It is also home to the Kodo drummers, whose exciting rhythms have become known worldwide. Their largest drum weighs more than half a ton. Each August, Kodo hosts an international arts festival on Sado; Earth Celebration is a wonderful melting pot of global arts, music and dance.

3 hours north of Tokyo by train and ferry, via Niigata; or by plane. Tourist information at Ryotsu ferry terminal. www.kodo.or.jp

Sapporo

The capital and cultural centre of Hokkaido, Sapporo is a spacious, gracious city with leafy boulevards and a nightlife area, Susukino, claimed by the locals to be the liveliest north of Tokyo. Among the hotels and department stores are Meiji-period brick and timber-frame buildings. The Clock Tower, the city's symbol, dates from 1878. It stands at the television tower end of Odori Park. During February, thousands of visitors

The serene caldera lake, Shikotsu, is ringed by volcanoes

flock to Odori Park to witness Hokkaido's major annual event, the Sapporo Yuki Matsuri (Sapporo Snow Festival), where artists carve huge, often intricate, ice sculptures.

The city is also home to the oldest brewery in Japan, established in 1876.

Hokkaido. 11 hours north of Tokyo by train via Morioka or 16 hours direct; also accessible by plane.
www.welcome.city.sapporo.jp

Sendai

The capital of the Tohoku region, Sendai is a brash, modern city, totally rebuilt after the war. Historically it is famous as the capital of Date Masamune, the powerful 17th-century warlord known as the 'one-eyed dragon', who dominated the north. You can see the massive walls of his castle, Aoba-jo, in Aobayama Park.
Tohoku. 2 hours north of Tokyo by train. Aoba-jo ruins. 20 minutes by bus; on foot turn west of station. Open: Tue–Sun 9am–4.15pm. Admission charge.

Shikotsu-Toya National Park

Lake Shikotsu and Lake Toya form the twin hearts of this beautiful national park, within easy reach of Sapporo. Here you can visit crater lakes, spas and active volcanoes and walk or climb amid glorious mountain scenery (*see p147*).
Hokkaido. Accessible by bus from Sapporo or Chitose airport; also by train from Sapporo or Chitose to Tomakomai, *then taxi to Lake Shikotsu, or to Toya for Lake Toya.*

Shiretoko Peninsula

Shiretoko has rugged volcanic scenery, and waterfalls of mineral-filled hot water, where you can bathe in natural pools in the rocks. You might encounter a bear in the mountains (*see p147*).
Hokkaido. A day's journey east of Sapporo, by express (change at Abashiri), slow train to Shari, then bus. Or hire a car at Abashiri.

Tono

The remote Tohoku villages, which together make up Tono, first sprang to fame in 1910, when a folklorist called Kunio Yanagida published a collection of strange, rather disturbing local legends, *Tono Monogatari*. These tales of malevolent water-sprites, demons and the outlandish ways of rural folk later appeared in English as *The Legends of Tono*, translated by Robert Morse. Ever since, visitors have gone to Tono in search of rustic peace. It is still a peaceful backwater (though gradually becoming spoilt), and you can still find waterwheels, and houses where people live under the same roof as their horses. The best way by far to explore the area is to hire a bicycle.
Tohoku. 1½ hours southeast of Morioka by train. Bicycle hire available near station.

Towada-ko (Lake Towada)

Tohoku's premier resort, Lake Towada is overrun with Japanese tourists in

buses in summer. It is nevertheless very beautiful – a large ancient caldera lake, deep and translucent, surrounded by rolling forested mountains. A popular walk is along pretty Oirase Gorge, but this is again very much set up for tourists. Tucked away in the hills round about are many old hot-spring inns.
Tohoku. 3 hours from Aomori and 2 hours from Hirosaki by bus.

Tsuruoka

A small, sleepy rural town, full of old farmers and wooden shopfronts, Tsuruoka is one of the gateways to Dewa Sanzan's sacred mountains (*see p67*). Wander the streets and visit **Chido Hakubutsukan** (Chido Museum), housed in the gracious old villa of the once-powerful Sakai family and other historic buildings.
Tohoku. 2 hours 35 minutes northwest of Sendai by train; also accessible from Niigata and Akita.
Chido Museum. Near castle, 10 minutes by bus from station. Tel: 0235 22 1199. Open: daily 9am–4.30pm. Admission charge.

Wakkanai

The windswept port of Wakkanai on the northernmost tip of Hokkaido is the ferry terminal for boats to the islands of **Rebun** and **Rishiri**, both remote and unspoilt and ideal for hikers (*see p147*).
Hokkaido. 7 hours by train north of Sapporo; or by plane. Daily ferries and flights on to Rishiri and Rebun.

Yamadera

At Yamadera, as the name ('Mountain Temple') suggests, the entire mountain is a temple. Scattered spectacularly across the steep wooded mountainside are small temples (some precariously balanced on stilts), stone images, and caves once the retreat of hermits. You climb the stone steps in company with many Japanese, who bring the ashes of their loved ones here to ensure that they will go to heaven. Inspired by the noisy whirr of the cicada, the poet Basho wrote one of his best-loved haiku here:
> *'The quiet –*
> *shrilling into the rocks*
> *the cicada's cry.'*

1 hour west of Sendai by train or 15 minutes from Yamagata.

Zao

Zao is a pretty little ski town on the Yamagata-Miyagi prefectural border. The stench of sulphur permeates everything, but it does mean that the *onsen* here are particularly good for your well-being. In winter, the snow falls thick on the fir trees and the winds blow strong, creating 'snow monsters' which are ethereal and beautiful to see – particularly at night. Take the ropeway to the mountain top for the best views. In summer, you can camp, hike or horse-ride, as well as visiting the Okama crater lake, whose waters change colour several times a day.
2¾ hours northwest of Tokyo by train.

The north

Central Japan

Central Japan is where the great dramas of Japanese history were played out; for over 1,000 years, this was the heart of the country. It's still where you'll find the most dazzling examples of traditional Japan, from the Zen monks raking their gravel to the geisha clip-clopping along cobbled streets, with World Heritage temples as stunning backdrops.

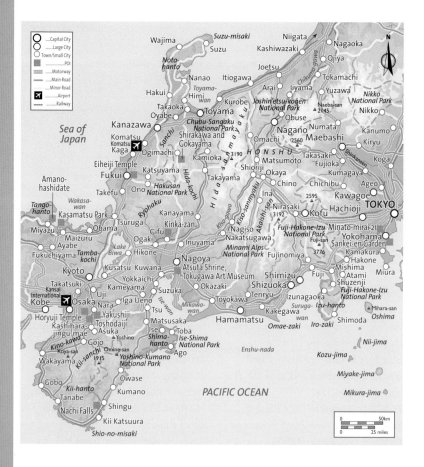

The old capital, Kyoto, will be the highlight of any visit to Japan; but the whole area is rich in history and culture. South of Kyoto is Nara, an older capital still, and the rolling hills of Asuka, where the ancient Japanese first settled in the 7th century. To the north are the Japan Alps and the rugged Sea of Japan coast. The area also includes three vibrant cities, Osaka, Kobe and Nagoya. Though Kobe was devastated in the January 1995 earthquake, rebuilding was completed within a few years.
Kyoto prefecture:
www.pref.kyoto.jp/visitkyoto/en

View across Kyoto from Kiyomizu Temple

KYOTO

Kyoto's history began in 794 when Emperor Kammu (737–806) made his new capital here. Home to the Japanese Imperial family from 794 to 1868, it was not always the capital city. Although Kamakura (1185–1333) and Edo, now Tokyo (1600–1867), served as Japan's capital, Kyoto remained the home and repository of classical culture.

Kyoto is well worth a long and leisurely visit, and exploring on foot. This is a living city, with industry and traffic-clogged streets, but you will soon discover the treasures hidden behind the modern façade. Japan's seventh-largest city boasts an extraordinary 1,600 temples, 400 shrines, a castle, a palace and some Imperial retreats of staggering beauty. UNESCO awarded World Heritage status to 14 spots within the city, and three more close by.

Kyoto escaped bombing during World War II, and there are streets full of mellow old houses and shops selling traditional handicrafts. The streets are laid out on a grid, making it easy to find your way around. Some sights are accessible only by bus, but a rudimentary subway system runs up the middle of the city.
1 hour from Kansai International Airport; 2½ hours west of Tokyo by train.

Daitokuji

Many people's favourite Zen temple, Daitokuji is a complex of 24 sub-temples, each with its own character, history and garden. Only a few are open to the public. Others you can enter to study Zen meditation, while some serve

Kyoto City Tourist Information Office
2nd Floor, JR Kyoto Station. Tel: 075 343 6655.
Open: daily 8.30am–7pm.

Several million worshippers visit the Fushimi Inari Shrine over Japanese New Year

Buddhist vegetarian meals. Daisen-in has the most famous garden – go early or late in the day to avoid the crowds and appreciate the exquisite perfection of the rocks, sand and moss that create a whole universe in a tiny space. Don't miss the beautiful ink paintings.

North Kyoto, a few minutes' bus ride from Kitaoji subway. Grounds always open. Sub-temples open: daily 9am– 4.30pm (last entry 4pm). Admission charge (variable).

Enryakuji

The atmospheric temple buildings of Enryakuji are in a splendid mountain setting, spread across the entire top of Mount Hiei. Enryakuji was founded in 806 to protect Kyoto from evil spirits, thought to come from the northeast. At its height there were 3,000 sub-temples, housing thousands of fierce warrior monks. In time the monks became a scourge rather than a blessing. Whenever they disagreed with the emperor, they would descend in force on the city, raiding rival monasteries, burning scriptures and killing the priests. Finally, in 1571, the warlord Nobunaga Oda stormed the mountain, burnt down the temples and killed the monks. More than 100 temples have been rebuilt. The majestic main hall, **Kompon Chu-do**, dates from 1642.

Northeast of Kyoto, bus from Kyoto station or Keihan Sanjo station. Tel: 077 578 0001. Grounds always open. Free admission. Kompon Chu-do. Open: daily 9am–4pm. Admission charge.

Fushimi Inari Taisha (Fushimi Inari Shrine)

This shrine, dating from the 8th century, is the most important of the almost 40,000 Shinto shrines dedicated to Inari, god of rice, sake and prosperity. Businessmen come in their thousands to pray for success and wealth.

The entire hillside is covered with more than 5,000 red *torii*, which are pressed together to form tunnels; you walk in a strange red twilight, occasionally emerging at a small shrine on a rocky outcrop.

South Kyoto, at Inari station.
Tel: 075 641 7331. Open: daily
8.30am–4pm. Free admission.

Ginkakuji (Silver Pavilion)

The exquisite Silver Pavilion is one of Kyoto's most famous sights – though in fact it was never silver. It was built as a pleasure villa for Shogun Yoshimasa in 1492, but Japan was so impoverished by civil war that there were no funds to cover the building in silver as planned. Instead it is of dark wood, with a phoenix perched on the roof. In front is a raked sand garden, and beyond that paths climb the wooded hillside, between waterfalls and ponds full of carp. Like his grandfather, Shogun Yoshimitsu Ashikaga, builder of the Golden Pavilion (*see pp86, 88*), Yoshimasa was a great patron of the arts. Within the temple grounds is the famous Dojin-sai, Japan's first ever tea ceremony room; apply in writing to view it.

East Kyoto, bus to Ginkakuji-michi.
Tel: 075 771 5725. Open: Mar–mid-Nov
daily 8.30am–5pm; 9am–4.30pm in
winter. Admission charge.

SHINTO SHRINES

You cannot be long in Japan without coming across a *torii*, the gateway that marks the entrance to a Shinto shrine and to the realm of the gods. Shrines are everywhere ('shrine' in this context means a Shinto place of worship, not a small household shrine): on mountain tops, in ancient cedar forests and beside lakes – also in Buddhist temples, in the middle of towns or on top of office blocks.

The Shinto deities – of which there are many – play a part in people's everyday lives. Each rules a different aspect of life, has a different animal messenger and inspires a different style of shrine architecture. Thus Inari, god of rice, prosperity and commercial success (many businessmen pray to him), has the fox as messenger and bright vermilion shrines.

Anyone can pray to the Shinto gods – for health, business success, a marriage partner or safety on the road. When you approach a shrine, first make sure to wash your hands and mouth to purify yourself and toss a coin into the offering box – a ¥5 coin is particularly auspicious. Then ring the bell which hangs above the shrine to wake the god, bow twice and clap your hands twice. This is the time to pray or make your wish. Afterwards bow twice again; when you step away, be careful not to turn your back on the shrine.

The oldest Shinto shrine is **Izumo** (*see p128*). The **Grand Shrines** at Ise (*see p103*), dedicated to the emperor, is considered the most important. The most famous is **Fushimi Inari Shrine** in Kyoto (*see above*).

Gion

Gion is Kyoto's legendary geisha
district. In the daytime, you can stroll
down Hanami-koji and admire the
17th-century restaurants and teahouses.
But the area really comes alive in the
early evening. Lanterns gleam, lights
glow softly behind the paper windows,
and you may see *maiko* – trainee geisha
– hurrying to work.
*Central Kyoto, 2 minutes east of Keihan-
Shijo station, off Shijo St.*

Gosho (Kyoto Imperial Palace)

At the heart of the city, the Imperial
Palace was the home of the emperor
until the mid-19th century. The austere
buildings, which date from 1855,
contrast with the lavishness of the
shogun's residence, Nijo Castle, just
down the road (*see pp89–90*). There are
several palaces within the compound,
linked by corridors or galleries and
separated by graceful gardens. The
Shishinden (Hall for State Ceremonies),
with its elaborate high throne, was
where the emperors were crowned.
*Central Kyoto, 10-min walk south of
Imadegawa subway. Tours organised
by Kunaicho (Imperial Household
Agency) near the gate (tel: 075 211
1215). http://sankan.kunaicho.go.jp.
Tours daily at 10am & 2pm.
Applications must be made in advance
via the Internet or by post. Completed
application form along with passport
necessary. Closed: Sat, Sun, national
holidays & 25 Dec–5 Jan.
Free admission.*

Heian Jingu (Heian Shrine)

Heian Shrine evokes the first Kyoto –
Heian-kyo, the Capital of Peace and
Tranquillity, founded in 794. The shrine
was built in 1895, and is dedicated to
the first and last emperors to reign in
Kyoto. Its brilliant vermilion buildings,
with their green-tiled roofs, are a two-
thirds scale replica of the original
Heian-period Imperial Palace. In
spring, people flock to see the cherry
blossoms in the beautifully landscaped
gardens.
*Central Kyoto, 10 minutes north of
Dobutsuen-mae bus stop. Open: daily,
mid-Mar–Aug 8.30am–6pm; early–
mid-Mar & Sept–Oct 8.30am–5.30pm;
Nov–Feb 8.30am–5pm. Admission charge
to garden; free admission to shrine.*

Katsura Rikyu (Katsura Imperial Villa)

The exquisite perfection of the Katsura
Imperial Villa with its elegant
landscaped gardens gives some idea of
the life of the aristocracy in the time of
the shoguns. Completed over 50 years,
beginning in 1590, the villa was built
for an aesthete brother of the emperor
and is considered one of the pinnacles
of Japanese architecture. There are
teahouses, moon-viewing pavilions, a
music room and a veranda for watching
kemari, a football game played at court.
The superb gardens were designed by
the great Japanese landscape architect
Kobori Enshu, who is said to have
accepted the job on two conditions:
unlimited time and unlimited funds.

Kyoto

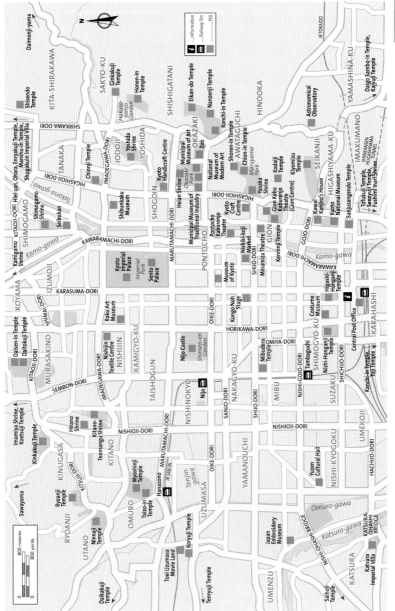

Southwest Kyoto, accessible by bus or train to Katsura station. Tours daily at 10am & 2pm. Visitors must be over 20 years old. Applications must be made in advance via the internet or by post. http://sankan.kunaicho.go.jp/order/index _EN.html. Closed: Sat, Sun, national holidays & 25 Dec–5 Jan. Free admission.

Kinkakuji (Golden Pavilion)

The fabulous Golden Pavilion is top of many visitors' sightseeing list for Kyoto. This also means large crowds, so an early visit is best. Surprisingly small and delicate, it perches on the edge of a lake, perfectly reflected in the water. The walls, pillars and eaves of the top two floors are entirely covered in gold leaf. On the pinnacle of the roof is a golden phoenix. Built in 1394, Kinkakuji was

YUKIO MISHIMA

Yukio Mishima (1925–70) is famous as much for his spectacular death as for his brilliant writing. The author of an enormous variety of intense, tormented novels, poetry and plays, Mishima published his first works when he was still at university. One of his most famous novels is *Kinkakuji* (*The Temple of the Golden Pavilion*), the true story of the monk who became obsessed with the beauty of the Golden Pavilion and burnt it down. Mishima ended his own life with a samurai-style seppuku (ritual suicide), having tried and failed to bring about a right-wing revolution.

originally a pleasure pavilion for Shogun Yoshimitsu. On his death, it was made into a Zen temple by his son. In 1950 a young monk burnt it to the ground; the present building is a faithful reconstruction.

The upper floors of Kinkakuji catch the light to bring out the full glory of their gold-leaf cladding

Machiya in Kyoto

Though World War II famously spared the picturesque city of Kyoto, the dynamic post-war years did not. As Japan transformed itself into a modern economic powerhouse, the bulldozers began tearing away at the city's historic architecture. The most obvious victims were the *machiya* – the wooden townhouses that acted as home, atelier and shopfront for the city's craftsmen and merchants. As beautiful as they were, the *machiya* were costly to maintain, with antiquated solutions to Kyoto's humid summers and cold winters.

But by the end of the 20th century, there was a clear shift towards preserving the *machiya*. Many were renovated and turned into cafés, bars, restaurants, diminutive museums and even luxury accommodation.

The old structures stand out for their distinctive wooden lattice doors, slatted *mushiko mado* (literally: 'insect cage windows'), and a long, narrow layout that stems from the days when properties were taxed by their width.

Stay
Iori Machiya
Renovated *machiya* can be rented by the night. At time of publication, Iori has ten properties, all epitomising luxury accommodation.
Tel: 075 352 0211.
www.kyoto-machiya.com/eng

Drink
Rocking Chair
Opened in 2009 and already a big name on Kyoto's bar scene, with vintage ports and exquisite cocktails.
Gokomachi-dori, Bukkoji-sagaru, Shimogyo-ku, Kyoto. Tel: 075 496 8679. www.bar-rockingchair.jp

Dine
Oku
Simple but superlative café fare. The *obanzai* (Kyoto-style home cooking) option is one of the best-value eats in Kyoto. No reservation necessary.
570–119 Gion-machi Minamigawa, Higashiyama-ku, Kyoto.
Tel: 075 531 4776.
www.oku-style.com

Traditional *machiya* in Kyoto's Gion district

Northwest Kyoto, near Ryoanji, accessible by bus. Tel: 075 461 0013. Open: daily 9am–5pm. Admission charge.

Kitano-Tenmangu (Shrine)

This splendid old shrine is dedicated to Sugawara-no Michizane, the 9th-century scholar who was deified as Tenjin, the god of learning (*see p137*). The gardens are planted with plum trees, his favourite plant, and there is a large bronze ox, his animal guardian. The shrine is particularly famous for its flea market, held on the 25th of each month. On that day the Tenjin Engi Scrolls, depicting the legend of Michizane, are on view.
Central Kyoto, north of Nijo Castle, accessible by bus. Open: Mar–Nov daily 9am–6pm (till 5.30pm in winter). Free admission.

Kiyomizu-dera (Temple)

No matter how many times you see Kiyomizu, you always come upon it with a sense of discovery. It is the most spectacular of structures, the vast thatched temple buildings standing on a scaffolding of immense wooden pillars, looking out across the city.

Kiyomizu ('Pure Water') was founded in 798. During its long and turbulent history it was burnt down several times; the present buildings date from 1633. The weather-worn temple buildings are immensely atmospheric. From the main hall, steps lead down to Otawa waterfall, whose pure waters give the temple its name and are said to have therapeutic properties. The small three-storeyed pagoda on the opposite hill gives a wonderful view of the whole temple.
East Kyoto, accessible by bus No 206 or 207 from JR Kyoto station, Gojo-zaka stop. 10-minute uphill walk from here. Tel: 075 551 1234. Open: daily 6am–6pm. Admission charge.

Kyoto Kokuritsu Hakubutsukan (Kyoto National Museum)

As one would expect in this city of temples, the Kyoto National Museum focuses on Buddhist art. The fine collection is shown in chronological order, beginning with ceramics and burial urns from the earliest historical periods, and includes a hall of gigantic bronze Buddhist images, black and white ink brush paintings, gold screens and calligraphy. Besides priceless Japanese works, there are Chinese ceramics and paintings, which were collected by temples and were often a major inspiration for local artists.
Southeast Kyoto, opposite Sanjusangendo. Tel: 075 541 1151. Open: Tue–Sun 9am–5pm (last entry 4.30pm). Admission charge.

Nanzenji

This famous and imposing Zen temple spreads across the foothills of Higashiyama, the 'Eastern Mountains'. Visitors come to study Zen, to dine on *yudofu* (simmered tofu, a Kyoto speciality served in small shops around the temple grounds) or simply to admire the buildings. Nanzenji's symbol is its massive two-storey gate, the Sanmon; from the upper floor there are fine views across the city. Its glory is the palatial abbot's quarters, once part of the Kyoto Imperial Palace, given to the temple in 1611. The many rooms are decorated with lavish paintings – ink paintings of bamboos and pine, paintings on gold leaf of tigers frolicking. At the centre is the Leaping Tiger garden, a serene space of raked sand and rocks, one of which resembles a leaping tiger.

East Kyoto, accessible by bus or tram to Keage station. Tel: 075 771 0365. Open: Mar–Nov daily 9am–5pm (till 4.30pm in winter). Admission to the grounds is free although some buildings have a small admission fee.

Nijo-jo (Nijo Castle)

Nijo Castle, with its sumptuous rooms full of paintings glimmering with gold leaf, was built in 1603 as the Kyoto residence of Ieyasu, the first Tokugawa shogun. You enter through the huge and ornately carved front gates, then pass through a series of audience chambers. Common people could go no further than the first, decorated with lavish paintings, friezes and coffered ceilings to impress upon them the shogun's power. The inner halls were for those of higher rank; here the

Nijo Castle's clean exterior hides a sumptuous treat of paintings and decoration inside

decoration is subtler but even more costly. Ever wary of treachery, the shoguns installed 'nightingale floors', which creak under the lightest tread to warn of intruders. There were no trees in the magnificent landscaped gardens: the shoguns did not want to see the falling leaves and be reminded of their own mortality.

Central Kyoto, bus or Oike subway. Tel: 075 841 0096. Open: daily 8.45am–5pm (last entry 4pm). Closed: 26 Dec–4 Jan & Tue in Jan, Jul, Aug & Dec. Admission charge.

Ninnaji

This grand old temple had a retired emperor as its first abbot and he was succeeded by Imperial princes until the Meiji era. Founded in 842, the temple burnt down and was rebuilt in the 1630s. The splendid main hall was originally part of the Imperial Palace and houses an image of the Buddha Amida from 888. The spacious grounds are full of cherry trees; people come in April to admire the blossom.

Northwest Kyoto, near Ryoanji, accessible by bus. Tel: 075 461 1155. Open: daily 9am–4.30pm (till 4pm in winter). Admission to the grounds is free but there is a fee for some temple buildings.

Nishi-Honganji

This is a much-loved, truly historic World Heritage Site. Some of Kyoto's most spectacular sights are hidden here. Visitors are free to explore the vast outer halls, built to accommodate thousands of worshippers, but to see the real treasures you must apply in advance. The inner chambers are breathtaking. Brought from Fushimi Castle, palace of the 16th-century warlord Hideyoshi Toyotomi, they are decorated in the lavish Momoyama style. Sliding doors open to reveal chamber after chamber, glowing with gold. Every surface of the screens, transoms and coffered ceilings is covered in gold leaf, painted with landscapes, pine trees and birds. The oldest Noh stage in existence, dating from 1581, is also here.

South Kyoto, 10-min walk northwest of Kyoto station. Tel: 075 371 5181. Open: daily 6am–5pm (varies according to season). Guided tours are available, although it is advisable to make reservations several days in advance. Free admission.

Ohara

From Kyoto a single road winds north through the hills to the tiny village of Ohara. **Jakko-in**, west of the village, is a secluded nunnery at the top of a long flight of rough stone steps, enclosed by steep hills. In 1185 the Empress Kenreimon-in was incarcerated here, after a long war in which she had seen her whole family killed and her baby son – the heir to the empire – drowned. The atmospheric old temple and mossy gardens are said to be exactly as they were in her day. **Sanzen-in Temple**, to the east, has beautiful grounds brilliant with colourful maple leaves in autumn.

The main hall houses three great 10th-century images: the Buddha Amida accompanied by two bodhisattvas. Try to avoid visiting during weekends in October and November, when it can get unbelievably crowded.

10km (6 miles) northeast of Kyoto, accessible by bus.
Jakko-in. Open: Mar–Nov daily 9am–5pm (till 4.30pm in winter; last entry 30 minutes before closing). Admission charge.
Sanzen-in Temple. Open: Mar–Nov daily 8.30am–5pm (till 4.30pm in winter). Admission charge.

Pontocho

At night, Pontocho is one of Kyoto's liveliest areas. This small pedestrian alley running alongside the river has some prohibitively expensive geisha establishments – it is Kyoto's number-two geisha district, after Gion (*see p84*) – but also plenty of cheaper, casual restaurants. In summer you can dine on a veranda over the river.

Central Kyoto, west of the river, between Keihan-Shijo and Keihan-Sanjo stations.

Ryoanji

The garden at Ryoanji, founded in 1450, is the ultimate Zen garden – an expanse of white sand, perfectly raked, surrounding 15 rocks. The best way to appreciate it is to sit quietly and let the meaning unfold. Don't miss the quiet graveyard behind the temple, with a lake and a view across Kyoto. Go early to avoid the crowds.

Northwest Kyoto, near Kinkakuji and Ninnaji, accessible by bus.
Tel: 075 463 2216. Open: Mar–Nov daily 8am–5pm; 8.30am–4.30pm in winter. Admission charge.

Saihoji

Entering Saihoji's moss garden is like stepping into an enchanted forest. Designed in 1339 by the great Zen priest Muso Soseki (*see* Tenryuji, *p98*), it was once as austere as Ryoanji's garden. Then moss began to grow. There are now more than 100 varieties, forming a richly textured carpet

Pontocho's neon lights are dazzling

Some of the 1,001 images of the deity Kannon in Sanjusangendo Temple

beneath the glowing maples and giving the place its popular name, Kokedera (Moss Temple).

However, its many visitors have begun to threaten the delicate garden, so application to see it must be made by postcard around a month in advance (Kyoto City Tourist Information Office has details – *see p81*). You pay a hefty admission charge and trace sutras (Buddhist scriptures) for one hour. But the garden makes it all worthwhile.

Southwest Kyoto, near Katsura, accessible by bus. Tel: 075 391 3631. Admission charge.

Sanjusangendo

This awe-inspiring temple, founded in 1164 and rebuilt in 1266 after it burnt down, is really a vast altar, with 1,001 images of Kannon, the deity of mercy, standing rank upon rank. The central image, a huge 1,000-armed Kannon (actually only 40 arms but equal in Buddhism to 1,000 as each arm serves 25 worlds), is particularly fine.

Southeast Kyoto, opposite National Museum. Tel: 075 561 3334. Open: Apr–mid-Nov daily 8am–5pm; 9am–4.30pm in winter. Admission charge.

Shugakuin Rikyu (Shugakuin Imperial Villa)

Set in the hills overlooking the city, the villa and its gardens – surely the most spectacular in Japan – were designed in the 1650s for the retired Emperor Go-Mizuno-o. Dotted about the grounds are pavilions and teahouses where he passed his days moon-gazing and composing poetry. From the streams and tinkling cascades of the Lower Garden, you climb along a tree-lined path to the Middle Garden. The pavilion here has a famous painting of fish, so lifelike that the artist painted a net over them to prevent them from swimming away. Finally you reach the Rin'un-tei ('Pavilion in the Clouds') and a breathtaking panorama. The Upper Garden – with its lake, bridges, waterfalls, islands and exquisite pavilions – forms the foreground; behind is the city of Kyoto, with range upon range of mountains.

Northeast Kyoto, en route to Ohara and Enryakuji, accessible by bus.
Tours at 9am, 10am, 11am, 1.30pm & 3pm Mon–Fri, 9am, 10am & 11am Sat. See p84 for booking details.
Free admission.

Toji

Originally built in 794, Toji's five-storey pagoda was rebuilt in 1643 after a series of fires destroyed four previous ones. At 57m (187ft) it is the tallest pagoda in the country and a symbol of Kyoto.

This splendid old temple houses some marvellous art, including a celebrated 9th-century three-dimensional mandala (Buddhist symbol of the universe) made up of 21 images. Toji is famous for its flea market, held on the 21st of each month.

Southern Kyoto, 15-minute walk southwest of station. Tel: 075 691 3325. Open: daily 8.30am–5.30pm (till 4.30pm in winter). Admission charge but entry to the temple grounds is free.

Saihoji's lush green surroundings

Beautiful Byodo-in, which was built to resemble a phoenix

KYOTO ENVIRONS

Some of Kyoto's most famous and ancient buildings are not in the city itself but some distance away to the south.

Uji

The small town of Uji is famous above all for its tea, considered the best in Japan. But 1,000 years ago, this pretty area – surrounded by gently rolling hills and on a rushing river, some 20km (12 miles) from Kyoto on the road to Nara – was where princes and nobles built their country villas. Later, many were turned into temples, of which one, the Byodo-in, survives.

Byodo-in (Phoenix Hall)

Look on your ¥10 coin and you will see the Byodo-in. This exquisite structure was built in 1053 and has survived in its pristine beauty for nearly 1,000 years. Designed as an earthly imitation of the Western Paradise, it was built to resemble a phoenix, revered in Japan as the protector of the Buddha. The two verandas, on delicate pillars, stretch to each side like wings, and the corridor at the back forms the tail. On the roof are two bronze phoenixes. The whole building stands, extraordinarily light and ethereal, poised above the surrounding lake.

The hall houses a statue of Amida, Buddha of compassion and ruler of the Western Paradise. Commoners were not allowed to enter, so the builders inserted a window in the latticework. From across the lake you can see Amida's face, perfectly framed, gazing benevolently out. The vast statue is made of wood, lacquered and gilded, surrounded by an intricately carved golden halo. Adorning the walls are 52 bodhisattvas, dating from the 11th century, seated on clouds, playing musical instruments. On the doors and wooden walls are delicate paintings, some of the oldest in Japan.

Within the temple complex, the Kannon-do dates from the 13th century and houses an image of Kannon, the deity of mercy. There is also a treasure house where you can see the weather-worn original phoenix finials.
10-minute walk from Uji station.
Tel: 0774 21 2861. Open: Mar–Nov daily 8.30am–5.30pm; 9am–4.30pm in winter.
Admission charge.

Daigoji

Daigoji's picturesque grounds spread across a mountainside and include Kyoto's oldest building, a five-storey pagoda (AD 951). You can stroll past temples and ponds, then climb the pilgrims' path to the temple buildings at the top of the hill.

The glory of the temple is a much later development, the sub-temple of **Sambo-in**. Remodelled in 1598 on the instructions of Toyotomi Hideyoshi

(*see p8*), **Sambo-in** is a supreme example of the great general's taste for opulence and luxury. Room after room is walled with exquisite painted screens. The whole complex focuses on the lavish garden.
Southeast of Kyoto, en route to Uji (20 minutes), 10-minute bus ride from Rokujizo station (alight at Samboin-mae). Tel: 075 571 0002. Grounds always open.
Sambo-in. Open: Mar–Oct daily 9am–5pm (till 4pm in winter).
Admission charge.

Mampukuji

Mampukuji is a Chinese Zen temple – one of the very few in Japan – founded by the Chinese Zen master Ingen in the 17th century and built in Ming-dynasty style. The temple buildings incorporate elements of Chinese design and contain images of vigorous plump-faced bodhisattvas like elderly cherubs, utterly unlike Japanese images. Mampukuji is a living, working monastery with a community of monks. It is also famous for its cuisine: if you book beforehand you can try Chinese Buddhist vegetarian dishes in the temple's dining hall.
South of Kyoto, en route to Uji, 5-minute walk from Obaku station. Tel: 0774 32 3900. Open: daily 9am–4.30pm. Admission charge.

Uji is 40–50 minutes south of Kyoto by train.

Walk: Higashiyama

This stroll through the picturesque backstreets of Higashiyama (the 'Eastern Mountains') in southeast Kyoto begins near the city's best-loved temple and ends at the huge and colourful Heian Shrine.

Allow 3 hours.

Take the bus to Umamachi, then walk round the block to Kawai Kanjiro's house, or take a taxi.

1 Kawai Kanjiro Kinenkan (Kawai Kanjiro's House)

Kawai Kanjiro (1890–1966) was a potter who produced wonderful, idiosyncratic works. Some of his pots are exhibited in his house, along with his folk art collection and kiln.
Tel: 075 561 3585. Open: Tue–Sun 10am–5pm. Closed: Mon & 10–20 Aug. Admission charge.
From the main road, Gojo-dori, cross under the expressway to Gojozaka, the narrow road beyond a large temple gate.

2 Kiyomizu Temple

Gojozaka – the quiet way to approach this most popular of temples – leads steeply uphill past a stonemason's workshop specialising in gravestones. Many walkers come to place flowers on graves; higher up, the hillside is covered in tombs. Walk up some steps and suddenly, magically, Kiyomizu Temple (*see pp86 & 88*) is before you.
From Kiyomizu, take Kiyomizu-michi, the street at the front gate of the temple.

3 Sannenzaka and Ninenzaka

Among the many souvenir shops are pottery shops specialising in Kiyomizu porcelain and stoneware. Watch for cobbled steps leading down to your right to Sannenzaka, a charming street lined with willow trees, old wooden shops, houses and small teahouses. Soon another set of steps, marked by a signpost in English for 'Maruyama Park', leads to your right, down to Ninenzaka, with craft shops and restaurants. At the end of Ninenzaka is a main road. On the hillside to your right you will see an enormous Buddha, a memorial to those who died in World War II.
Cross the main road and walk north to Maruyama Park. A red torii on your left marks the entrance to Yasaka Shrine.

4 Yasaka Jinja (Yasaka Shrine)

Yasaka's red-painted buildings are particularly evocative in the evening, lit with thousands of paper lanterns. This splendid old shrine serves the nearby

Gion area (*see p84*) and organises the annual Gion festival (*see p17*).
Return to Maruyama Park and walk on northwards.

5 Heian Jingu (Heian Shrine)

Your walk takes you past the huge, ornately carved Sanmon Gate of **Chion-in Temple**, the largest temple gate in Japan. Beyond Chion-in is **Shoren-in Temple**, which has two beautiful gardens. Cross Sanjo-dori, with its tram lines leading into the centre of town. Ahead of you is a huge *torii*. Cross the painted bridge to Heian Shrine (*see p84*).

Chion-in Temple. Tel: 075 531 2111. Open: daily 9am–4pm. Admission charge.
Shoren-in Temple. Tel: 075 561 2345. Open: daily 9am–4.30pm. Admission charge.
Take the bus back to the city centre or the station. Or cut back towards the hills, to Nanzenji; from there follow the Philosopher's Path to Ginkakuji.

Walk: Higashiyama

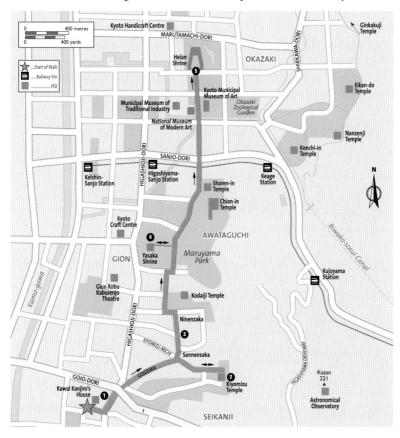

Walk: Arashiyama

This is a gentle stroll through bamboo groves at the foot of the Arashiyama hills in western Kyoto, taking in old temples, a hermitage and a splendid Imperial Palace-turned-temple. In autumn, the maple trees are a blaze of colour.

Allow half a day.

Take a bus or train to Arashiyama. From Togetsu-kyo (Moon-crossing Bridge), you can take a punt down the river. Walk away from the river; Tenryuji is on your left.

1 Tenryuji

The temple was founded in 1339 on the former site of Emperor Go-Daigo's villa, after a priest dreamed of a dragon rising from the nearby river – *ten-ryu* means 'heavenly dragon'. The original

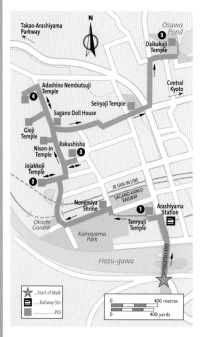

buildings have disappeared but the celebrated 14th-century garden remains. This was designed by the great Zen Buddhist monk, teacher and poet Muso Soseki (1275–1351). At the centre is a lake shaped like the character for 'heart', surrounded by raked sand, rocks and pines, with the hills of Arashiyama as the backdrop.
Tel: 075 881 1235. Open: daily 8.30am–5.30pm. Admission charge.
From the back (north) exit, follow the path through a bamboo grove. The road goes uphill and round to the right, past a small pond to another old wooden gate.

2 Jojakkoji

The atmospheric old temple belongs to the Nichiren sect of Buddhism (*see box on p76*). You can wander the cobbled paths along mossy tree-clad slopes, dotted with weathered wooden buildings. In autumn, the colours of the leaves make Jojakkoji especially lovely.

Tel: 075 861 0435. Open: daily 9am–4.30pm. Admission charge.
Take the first paved road on your left; turn right just beyond a vegetable field. Rakushisha is on your left.

3 Rakushisha

This idyllic little hut, with its steep thatched roof, paper doors and decorative bamboo fence, was where the poet Basho stayed when he visited Kyoto. Looking out on to the hills of Arashiyama, he wrote one of his last works, *Saga Diary*.
Open: daily 9am–5pm.
Admission charge.
Return to the road and follow it past several temples (about 10 minutes). Carry on up as the road becomes narrower and steeper. Cobbled steps lead off to your left to Nembutsuji.

4 Adashino Nembutsuji

This hushed, rather haunting temple is packed with gravestones. Centuries ago, Adashino was a burial ground for all the nameless common folk not grand enough to be honoured with a tomb. The many stone Buddhas scattered around the countryside were assembled here so that prayers could be offered for their souls.
Tel: 075 861 2221. Open: Mar–Nov daily 9am–5pm; 9.30am–4pm in winter. Admission charge.
Retrace your steps and take the main road on your left. Follow the road round past Seiryoji to Daikakuji.

5 Daikakuji

Daikakuji was built as a palace for the 9th-century Emperor Saga, who converted it into a temple. Pressed against the mountainside, it overlooks a limpid lake, **Osawa Pond**. The present, still palatial, buildings date from the 16th century. You can stroll along the broad verandas beneath the spreading eaves, admire the sliding doors covered in gold leaf and painted with peonies and plum trees, and feed the carp in Osawa Pond.
Tel: 075 871 0071. Open: daily 9am–4.30pm. Admission charge.
From Daikakuji there are buses back to Kyoto station and central Kyoto. Bus: 28.

Crowds stroll along the Hozu River in Arashiyama, 'Storm Mountain'

Central Japan

Fukui

Eiheiji

This ancient and famous Zen temple was founded in 1244 by Dogen, who brought the Zen teachings from China to Japan. It is a living, working temple, where Zen monks meditate, sleep, garden and eat simple vegetarian meals. Eiheiji provides a glimpse of this austere lifestyle.

The temple complex is arranged with impressive symmetry across the lower slopes of a mountain. The three most important rooms, where monks are forbidden to speak, are the toilet, the bath and the living and meditating quarters. There is also a splendid Buddha Hall, which enshrines images of the three Buddhas of past, present and future; an imposing main gate,

The spacious halls of the ancient Eiheiji Zen Temple, where monks still live

BASHO AND HAIKU

Matsuo Basho (1644–94) was the quintessential Japanese poet. Born in Iga Ueno, he soon left his native town and took up the life of a wanderer. Like a Zen monk, he owned nothing and never married. His greatest achievement was to take the 17-syllable haiku, one of the classic forms of Japanese poetry, and make it into a fine art. Basho's finest haiku encapsulate a moment and all its philosophical ramifications in just a few words, as in the famous

'Old pond,
frog jumps in –
sound of water.'

with carved guardian deities; and the mausoleum, containing the ashes of Dogen. There is also a large wooden block where disciples bang their head to reawaken themselves; there is now a large hole that has worn into it over hundreds of years.

Many Westerners come here for a taste of Zen training for a few days, a few weeks – or a few years. To do so, apply (by telephone or in writing) at least two weeks in advance. Eiheiji is periodically closed. Phone or check with the local TIC for more information.

Fukui. 50 minutes southwest of Kanazawa; 1½ hours northeast of Kyoto by train. Eiheiji is 35 minutes east of Fukui by train. Eiheiji-cho, Yoshida-gun, Fukui-ken. Tel: 0776 63 3631. Open: daily dawn–5pm. Admission charge.

Gifu

Gifu, surrounded by wooded hills, is a small, pleasant city spreading across the valley of the River Nagara. It is famous for cormorant fishing. Every fine night between 11 May and 15 October, fishermen in traditional grass skirts and peaked black hats drift downriver in small boats. Small, sweet trout – a delicacy – are attracted by the light of torches, and the cormorants dive in, catch the fish, and are then yanked back to the boat by a leash around their necks.

Gifu also has the largest lacquer Buddha in Japan and two fine country temples, tucked away at the end of tram lines: **Tanigumi**, deep in the mountains, and **Yokokura**, famous for its mummified priests. From the park you can catch a cable car to the top of **Kinka-zan** (mountain), where there is a small reconstruction of Gifu's old castle.

30 minutes north of Nagoya by train. www.pref.gifu.lg.jp.

Cormorant fishing. Tickets available from hotels or directly (tel: 058 262 0104).

Tanigumi and Yokokura temples. 30–45 minutes by tram from Chusetsu Bridge terminal, Gifu. Open: daily 9am–5pm. Free admission to grounds; admission charge to see the mummies.

Eiheiji is a quintessential Zen temple, designed for simple living

Hikone

As you walk from the station through Hikone's quiet streets, you can see the beautiful old castle on the hill in front of you. Completed in 1622, it took nearly 20 years to build and is one of the finest castles in Japan. Much of the original, with its graceful structure and sweeping roofs, is still intact. From the upper floors you can look out across the placid waters of Lake Biwa. In spring, the park surrounding the castle is pink with cherry blossom. There is also an elegant landscaped garden, **Genkyuen.**

50 minutes northeast of Kyoto by train.
Castle. 10-minute walk west of station.
Tel: 0749 22 2742.
Open: daily 8.30am–5pm.
Admission charge.

Iga Ueno

In feudal times, the out-of-the-way town of Iga Ueno was the headquarters of the ninja (*see box*). Here they posed as farmers, living in farmhouses riddled with false floors, walls that were really revolving doors, hidden rooms and hoards of concealed weapons. One of these houses remains, its secrets revealed by young women clad in ninja outfits. Iga Ueno is also the birthplace of Japan's best-loved poet, Matsuo Basho.

1 hour east of Nara; 1½ hours southwest
of Nagoya by train.
Ninja House: in Ueno Park.
Open: daily 9am–5pm.
Admission charge.

NINJA

Spies and hired killers, the ninja were masters of the art of invisibility. They could travel at astonishing speed, could climb supposedly impregnable castle walls, and used a fearsome battery of weapons. No matter how well protected you thought you were, a ninja, dressed head to toe in black, might suddenly swing in through a window or hurl a barbed chain dipped in poison to wrap around your neck. *Ninjutsu* (the art of stealth) flourished in the 14th and 15th centuries, and is still being taught today, though you are unlikely to meet a real-life ninja.

Inuyama

Inuyama Castle (1440) is Japan's oldest. A charming, small castle with thick wooden beams and low-slung rafters, it was made entirely without nails. From the top floor there are fine views of the pretty town of Inuyama and Kiso River. Nearby is **Uraku-en garden**, with its exquisite teahouse.

Not far away is **Meiji-mura**, a village of Meiji-period buildings, moved here to preserve them. There is an old kabuki theatre, a bathhouse, merchants' houses, a steam train and tram, and the entrance to Frank Lloyd Wright's original Tokyo Imperial Hotel, which survived the 1923 Tokyo earthquake.

25 minutes north of Nagoya by train.
Castle. 10-minute walk west of station.
Tel: 0568 61 1711. Open: daily 9am–5pm
(last entry 4.30pm).
Uraku-en garden. 5-minute walk from
castle. Tel: 0568 61 4608.
Open: Mar–Nov daily 9am–4pm.
Meiji-mura. 15 minutes from Inuyama

by train and bus; 1 hour from Nagoya by direct bus. Tel: 0568 67 0314. Open: Mar–Oct daily 10am–5pm; Tue–Sun 9.30am–4pm in winter.
Admission charge to each.

Ise

Ise's Grand Shrines is among the most important of Japan's Shinto structures and once a major destination for pilgrims. It houses the sacred mirror, one of the three Imperial regalia, and the emperor worships here after his enthronement.

Following Shinto tradition, the shrine is rebuilt afresh every 20 years, exactly as it was when first erected countless centuries earlier (the last, and 61st, rebuilding was in 1993). Ise is the only shrine which preserves this tradition.

Geku (Outer Shrine), traditionally established in 478, is dedicated to the goddess of agriculture and industry. Gravel paths lead through an ancient forest to the shrine buildings. As is usual in Shinto, you cannot enter the abode of the gods, but you can see the buildings beyond the fence.

Naiku (Inner Shrine) is a bus ride from Geku, at the top of a street of shops lining the ancient pilgrimage route. After crossing a bridge of unpainted cypress, you come to a place where pilgrims wash in the sacred Isuzu River. The shrine buildings, of plain unvarnished wood, are perfect reproductions of 6th-century Japanese architecture, and said to be modelled

on ancient storehouses. Amaterasu, the sun goddess and mythical ancestor of the Imperial family, is believed to be enshrined here (*see* Takachiho, *p144*).
1½ hours south of Nagoya by train. Geku. 10-minute walk west of station. Naiku. 15 minutes by bus from Geku. Open: daily dawn–dusk.
Free admission.

Izu-hanto (Izu Peninsula)

Izu is a beautiful peninsula southwest of Tokyo. It feels a million miles away, with its rolling green hills, dramatic landscapes and pristine beaches.

(*Cont. on p106*)

Hikone Castle in autumn

Religion

The concept of religion in Japan, and China, is markedly different from that in Western and Islamic societies where religion is connected with the concept of an exclusive faith. For most of Japanese history the two main religions, Shinto and Buddhism, have not been seen as mutually exclusive (today marriages are almost always conducted according to Shinto rituals while funerals are usually Buddhist).

The Meiji period (1868–1945) is one where this mutual coexistence

A knotted rope marking out sacred ground

broke down. As a result of rampant nationalism, 'State Shinto' was made the state religion and severe restrictions were placed on Buddhism. State Shinto was abolished after Japan's defeat in World War II and the normal harmony between Shinto and Buddhism was restored.

The indigenous religion of Japan is Shinto, the 'way of the gods', which is generally held to have grown out of an awe of aspects of nature. The basic concept of Shinto is that *kami* (a term that is often translated as God/gods, spirit or spirits though there is no precise equivalent in English) manifest themselves as aspects of nature, such as the sun, mountains, rocks, certain animals or trees. The principles of fertility and growth are also considered manifestations of *kami*. Each Shinto shrine is considered the residence of one or more *kami* and the priests conduct rites to these *kami* with the aim of maintaining a good relationship between the spirits and humanity.

Shinto is a religion without a founder or a canon and is not a religion in the Western sense, as you cannot convert to it. Instead, it is an

Five hundred Rakan statues, representing Shaka Nyorai's disciples, line the steps of the Buddhist Daisho-in temple on Mount Misen

amalgamation of Japanese myths, such as those contained in the *Kojiki* (records of ancient matters) and the *Nihon Shoki* (chronicle of Japan) which were both written in the 8th century, and the beliefs and practices of local communities.

Buddhism, which originated in 6th-century BC India, reached Japan in the 6th century AD. As Buddhism evolved in Japan it interacted with the indigenous Shinto and acquired a distinctive Japanese character. Initially Buddha was considered a *kami* from China and in the 8th century *kami* were included in Buddhist temples as protectors of the Buddhas. This interaction continued until ultimately

kami were considered as incarnations of bodhisattvas (Buddhas who delay liberation from the cycle of rebirth to help others). Buddhist statues were included on Shinto altars and statues of *kami* were made to represent Buddhist priests.

Buddhism, particularly Zen Buddhism, has had a pervasive influence on the aesthetic life of Japan. Some of the most typical and admired Japanese arts, such as the tea ceremony, landscape gardening, flower arranging and ink painting, are heavily influenced by the principles of Zen. This is amply illustrated in the simplicity, understatement and asymmetry that characterise these arts.

Aside from being famous for its beaches, Izu is well known for its *onsen*. **Shuzenji town** is probably one of the better-known places on the peninsula, thanks to its own *onsen* and its temple, **Shuzenji**, which is one of the oldest in this part of Japan at 1,200 years old. Shuzenji town is also known for its charm. **Izunagaoka** is another nearby *onsen* town that is worth a visit for its open-air *onsen* and pretty vistas.

Further south lies **Shimoda**, a bohemian beachside town popular with surfers for the waves and beach-goers for the stretch of white sand. Shimoda is also famous as the port of entry for the American Fleet in the 19th century.

Shuzenji. 2 hours southwest of Tokyo by train.
Shuzenji temple. Tel: 0558 72 0053.
Izunagaoka. 2¹/₂ hours southwest of Tokyo by train.
Shimoda. 3 hours southwest of Tokyo by train.

Kanazawa

This lively, attractive city is the cultural and business centre of the Sea of Japan coast. In the time of the shoguns, it was the capital of the hugely wealthy Maeda clan, whose patronage made it a centre for Noh theatre and for sumptuous crafts: *yuzen* dyeing for formal kimonos, Kutani porcelain, gold leaf and lacquerware.

Kanazawa escaped bombing in World War II, and much of the elegant old city, with its tiled roofs, remains. You can stroll the winding streets of

Former teahouses in the geisha quarter of Kanazawa now serve as bars and restaurants

Nagamachi, the old samurai area, and explore the pleasure quarters where you may still glimpse a geisha. The city's most famous sights are the legacy of the Maeda lords.

Ishikawa Kenritsu Bijutsukan (Ishikawa Prefectural Art Museum)

This excellent museum contains many of the Maeda treasures – golden saddles and stirrups, the finest Kutani porcelain, and a life-sized pheasant incense burner.

Opposite Kenroku-en and Seisonkaku. Tel: 076 231 7580. Open: daily 9.30am–4.30pm. Admission charge.

Ishikawa-mon (Ishikawa Gate)

Ishikawa Gate, virtually all that remains of Kanazawa Castle, gives some idea of how splendid the castle must have been.

At the entrance to Kanazawa University, opposite Kenroku-en.

Kenroku-en Garden

This glorious private garden of the Maeda family, traditionally rated one of Japan's three most beautiful, was completed over a period of 200 years. It is composed to form a series of pictures – 'Misty Lake', with its tortoise-shaped island and 'Morning Glory Teahouse', a waterfall plunging through woodland.
15 minutes by bus from station. Tel: 076 234 3800. Open: Mar–mid-Oct daily 7am–6pm; 8am–4.30pm in winter. Admission charge.

Seisonkaku Villa

In 1863 the 13th Maeda lord built Seisonkaku as a retirement villa for his mother. The villa is the last word in opulence, full of exquisite ornamentation, with gold leaf dusting the sliding doors and coffered ceilings.
Beside Kenroku-en. Tel: 076 221 0580. Open: Thur–Tue 9am–5pm (last entry 4.30pm). Admission charge.

Kanazawa is 2¼ hours northeast of Kyoto and 4½ hours northwest of Tokyo by train; or fly to Komatsu Airport. For information contact: Kanazawa International Exchange Foundation, 1-5-3 Honmachi (tel: 076 220 2522); also tourist information office in station.

Kobe

Although devastated in the January 1995 earthquake, the port city of Kobe is now largely back to normal. It is famous for its cosmopolitan flavour. Many of the first Westerners who came to Japan in the 19th century made their homes on the pleasant slopes of Mount Rokko and, with Chinese and Indian merchants, formed a busy international community. You can visit some of their houses in the Kitano-cho area, or take a cable car to the top of Rokko for views across the city and the Inland Sea.
15 minutes by ferry from Kansai International Airport; 15 minutes from Osaka and 30 minutes from Kyoto by train.

Koya-san (Mount Koya)

During the 1600s there were about 1,500 monasteries around Koya-san, but in the 17th century the Tokugawa shogunate clamped down on the economic power of the priests, seizing

The famous stone lantern links earth and water in Kenroku-en Garden

Central Japan

Framed by the hills and trees, Matsumoto Castle's pagoda makes an impressive picture

land and destroying temples. This land confiscation continued during the Edo period by the government, who favoured the practice of Shinto. Today, Koya-san is a centre of Japanese Buddhism, with more than 110 temples. A quintessential Japanese experience is a night in a Buddhist temple on Mount Koya, centre of the Shingon sect, established by the priest and teacher Kobo Daishi. He founded the first monasteries on this mountaintop plateau in 816. In the Sacred Precinct is the Great Pagoda, the symbol of Koya-san; nearby **Kongobuji**

has sumptuous 16th-century painted screens. Most impressive of all is the 1.5km (1-mile) long cemetery, shaded by ancient cedars, where nearly every important person in Japanese history is buried. If you stay in a temple, you will be served lavish vegetarian cuisine and be awakened by the 5am call to prayers. *1½ hours south of Osaka by train. Koya-san Tourist Association. Tel: 0736 56 2616. www.shukubo.jp*

Matsumoto
The black walls and tiled turrets of Matsumoto Castle rising above

a lily-covered moat, with the snow-covered peaks of the Japan Alps as the backdrop, are a truly breathtaking sight. Completed in 1597, this is one of Japan's finest castles, second only to Himeji Castle (*see p126*) in beauty and elegance of form. It was built to withstand real warfare and there are chutes for bombarding attackers and slots for arrows. The castle also has an exquisite 'moon-viewing turret'.

2 hours northeast of Nagoya by train; also accessible by plane.
Matsumoto Castle. 20-minute walk northeast of station. Open: mid-Jul–Aug daily 8.30am–6pm (till 5pm Sept–early Jul). Admission charge.

Nagano

Nagano is the gateway to the Japan Alps and some of the most splendid countryside in Japan; people come to ski, hike and take the waters in the area's famous hot-spring resorts. It also hosted the Winter Olympics in 1998. Meanwhile, pilgrims come to worship at **Zenkoji**, a Buddhist temple founded in the 7th century. Follow the line of pilgrims shuffling into the dark recesses and you will be able to put your hand on the large, heavy key known as the 'key of paradise', believed to ensure salvation if touched.

2½ hours northwest of Tokyo by train. Zenkoji. 1.5km (1 mile) from station. Always open. Free admission to temple; admission charge for inner sanctum and 'key of paradise'.

Nagoya

Nagoya is Japan's fourth-largest city (though most people from Nagoya call it the centre of Japan), a major industrial metropolis; much of the nation's car industry is in the area. A centre for the aircraft and munitions industries during World War II, it was bombed flat. Today it is a large, vibrant city with modern buildings and wide streets – not beautiful, but with plenty of energy and life.

Nagoya was the birthplace of Japan's three great 16th-century warlords, the last of whom, Tokugawa Ieyasu (*see box on p74*), succeeded in unifying Japan. He built a formidable castle here in 1612, of which the present castle is a faithful reconstruction. Also visit **Atsuta Shrine**, one of the three most important in Japan, repository for the Sacred Grass-mowing Sword, part of the Imperial regalia, and the **Tokugawa Art Museum**, which contains the collection of the Tokugawa family.

2 hours west of Tokyo by train. For information contact: Nagoya International Centre (tel: 052 581 0100). Nagoya Castle. 5-minute walk from Shiyakusho subway. Tel: 052 231 1700. Open: daily 9am–4.30pm. Admission charge.
Atsuta Shrine. 5 minutes by train from Nagoya station. Always open. Free admission.
Tokugawa Art Museum. 20 minutes by bus from station. Tel: 052 935 6262. Open: Tue–Sun 10am–5pm. Admission charge.

NARA

The small city of Nara saw the first brilliant flowering of Japanese culture in the 8th century. Today it is a pleasant place set amid lush countryside, given over almost entirely to the celebration of its history. Much of the city is parkland where deer roam freely (and appear in the most unexpected places).

Initially the Japanese moved their capital to a new site whenever the emperor died, to avoid pollution by his death. Then, in the 8th century, as their society became more complex, they planned a great and permanent capital. The site they chose was Nara,

and the city was founded in 710. It was built on a grid plan, like the capital of neighbouring China, its splendid white-walled buildings embellished with vermilion pillars and green-tiled roofs.

In the new capital culture and the arts flourished, underpinned by Buddhist faith. The culmination was the building of Todaiji, with its colossal Great Buddha, the largest bronze image in the world. When the image was unveiled, foreign potentates from along the Silk Road came bearing gifts to attend the ceremony.

But in 784 the powerful Fujiwara family, who dominated Japan, decided

Nara

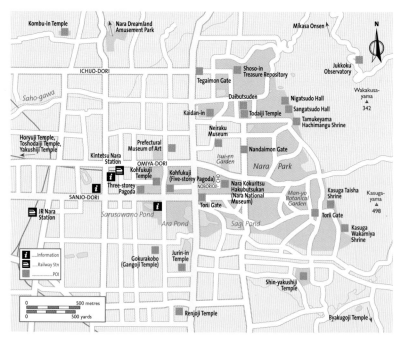

to move the capital again – briefly to Nagaoka and then to Kyoto. Nara was subsequently left outside the mainstream of history; as a result, while Kyoto burnt down again and again, several of Nara's temples and works of art – the legacy of a mere 74 years as capital – have survived for over 1,200 years, testimony to the glory of this ancient capital.

Nara is small enough to cover on foot; or you can hire a bicycle. The main sights are fairly close together in and near the deer park.
30 minutes–1 hour south of Kyoto by train.

For information contact: Nara City Tourist Centre (tel: 0742 22 3900); also in Nara and Kintetsu Nara stations.

Kasuga Taisha Shrine
A multitude of stone lanterns (1,780 in all) lines the steps leading up to the grand vermilion halls of Kasuga Taisha Shrine. This famous shrine was founded in the 8th century by the immensely powerful Fujiwara family to be the guardian shrine of the new capital. Until the middle of the 19th century it was rebuilt every 20 years, according to Shinto custom (*see* Ise, *p103*). The present buildings (1863) still faithfully follow the Heian style. The shrine is famous for performances of sacred dance. The **treasure house** contains masks and drums used in dancing, and other ritual objects.
In the deer park. Shrine always open.

Free admission.
Treasure house. Open: daily 9am–4pm.
Admission charge.

Kohfukuji
Kohfukuji's five-storey pagoda is the symbol of Nara. Founded in the 8th century along with Kasuga Shrine, Kohfukuji was the Fujiwara family temple and guardian temple of the capital. Not one of the original 175 buildings remains, all having been burnt to the ground; the buildings seen today are all later reconstructions. The

The 15th-century reconstructed pagoda of Kohfukuji Temple (8th century)

five-storey pagoda dates from 1426 and the nearby three-storey pagoda from 1143. Several of the halls can be entered. To see Kohfukuji's beautiful Buddhist sculptures, you will have to visit the **treasure house**.

Central Nara. Tel: 0742 22 7755.
www.kohfukuji.com.
Grounds always open. Free admission.
Treasure house. Open: daily 9am–5pm.
Admission charge.

Nara Kokuritsu Hakubutsukan (Nara National Museum)

The Nara Museum has a fine collection of works of art produced during the first flowering of Buddhism in Japan. The displays are organised according to the different Buddhist schools and include sculptures, calligraphy and paintings. The most priceless treasures are kept in the Shoso-in, a repository within the grounds of Todaiji (*see below*), with temperature and humidity carefully regulated. These are the gifts brought from as far afield as ancient Persia to Emperor Shomu on the founding of Todaiji, and include Silk Road ceramics, textiles and glassware. Usually the treasures are not on view, but once a year, for two weeks in late October and early November, some are displayed in the Nara Museum; at that time the grounds of the Shoso-in are also open.

50 Noborioji-cho, just beyond Kohfukuji.
Tel: 0742 22 7771. www.narahaku.go.jp.
Open: Tue–Sun 9.30am–5pm (last entry 4.30pm). Admission charge.

Shin-yakushiji

Down a quiet street to the south of the deer park, with pleasant views across the surrounding hills, is ancient Shin-yakushiji. Founded in 747 by Empress Komyo to ensure her husband's recovery from illness, the 8th-century main temple building survives. It houses a wooden image of the Buddha of Healing, surrounded by 12 splendid *junishinsho* (guardian deities).

Just south of the deer park.
Tel: 0742 22 3736. Open: daily
9am–5pm. Admission charge.

Todaiji

Nara's Great Buddha is one of the most famous and important sights in Japan. The temple which houses the image, the 'Eastern Temple', is the largest wooden structure in the world, at 48m (157ft) high a notable feat of engineering.

After several attempts, the Great Buddha was successfully cast in 745. It represented the apogee of the glorious culture of the Nara court and was unveiled with great ritual and ceremony in 752. The image is of Vairocana Buddha, the essential Buddha, of whom all others are aspects. In the grounds is the Ordination Hall, which contains four famous 8th-century clay images of the guardians of the four directions.

Within deer park.
Tel: 0742 22 5511. Open: daily, Apr–Sept
7.30am–5.30pm; Oct 7.30am–5pm;
Nov–Feb 8am–4.30pm; Mar 8am–5pm.
Admission charge.

NARA ENVIRONS

Moving south from Nara you travel ever further back in time, to the very beginnings of Japanese civilisation at Asuka (*see p123*). The high point of any exploration of the Nara environs is undoubtedly the ancient temple complex at Horyuji. Much is made of the fact that Horyuji is the world's oldest wooden structure. What is said less often is that it provides a rare chance to breathe the air of a long-vanished world.

Horyuji

In a small town a few kilometres southwest of Nara is a complex of temples and pagodas which has stood for nearly 1,400 years. Horyuji was founded in 607 by Shotoku Taishi

Nara National Museum is a mixture of architectural styles

(Prince Shotoku), a leading figure in ancient Japanese history. A philosopher prince, he united the Japanese people under the rule of the emperor, and made Buddhism the national religion. Under his guiding hand, Japan developed a culture that rivalled China's. The pinnacle of his work was Horyuji.

What we see today at Horyuji is ancient weathered buildings, perfectly proportioned, which would have been brilliantly painted in Prince Shotoku's time, the orange pillars, white walls and green shutters designed to dazzle visiting envoys from China and Korea.

The buildings of the Western Precinct house ancient and beautiful images, in style close to the Buddhist art found along the Silk Road. There are serene bronze Buddhas, their eyes closed in meditative bliss, and exquisitely delicate paintings adorning the eaves of the main temple.

Within the treasure house are objects which give some idea of the opulence of aristocratic life in those days. Look in particular for the Tamamushi Tabernacle, an altar which belonged to an empress and was originally entirely covered in the iridescent wings of millions of *tamamushi* jewel beetles (sadly, the wings have long since rotted away).

Lastly you reach the Hall of Dreams, built to appease Prince Shotoku's soul

The beautifully reconstructed buildings of the Yakushiji complex

after his death. Within this elegant octagonal building is the Hidden Statue, a lifesize image of Prince Shotoku, worshipped as the Kuse Kannon, the Buddhist Saviour. Protected within its shrine for many centuries, the statue is perfectly preserved. Even now it is hidden for most of the time, only on view annually between 11 April and 5 May and 22 October and 3 November.

10 minutes from Nara by train and bus. Tel: 0745 75 2555. Open: Mar–mid-Nov daily 8am–5pm (till 4.30pm in winter; last entry 1 hour before closing). Admission charge.

Toshodaiji

This beautiful monastery complex was founded in 759 by the Chinese priest Ganjin, who had been invited to Japan by Emperor Shomu to tighten up monastic training. Many of the original buildings still stand, including the graceful Main Hall, with its unusual rounded pillars. The hall contains a striking image of Vairocana, the Cosmic Buddha, with a thousand tiny Buddhas forming the halo. There is also a wonderful lacquered statue of the blind old priest Ganjin himself in the Miei-do Hall, which is shown only once a year on 6 June, the anniversary of Ganjin's death.

5-minute walk from Nishinokyo station; 15 minutes south of Nara by train. Open: daily 8.30am–5pm (last entry 4pm). Admission charge.

Yakushiji

Yakushiji was founded a few decades after Horyuji, in 680. The only original building is the graceful East Pagoda; the West Pagoda and Main Hall are recent reconstructions, as faithful as possible to the originals and painted in the same brilliant vermilion, white and green. Yakushiji contains some of the finest and most famous works of the period, notably the Yakushi Trinity – statues of the Lord of the Eastern Paradise and his two attendants.

Close to Nishinokyo station, 10 minutes from Toshodaiji. Open: daily 8.30am–5pm. Admission charge.

Noto-hanto (Noto Peninsula)

Noto, the small peninsula shaped like a crooked finger which juts into the Sea of Japan north of Kanazawa, is famous for its remote and unspoilt beauty. Here, terraced paddy fields stretch down to the sea and local fishermen hang out their nets to dry. Nowadays there are good roads and summer visitors come to fish and swim, but seconds away from the road the pace of life is as slow as ever. The centre of the area is the fishing port of Wajima. Here, you can visit the outdoor market where local women sell fish and vegetables, buy the peninsula's famous lacquerware and watch a performance of demon-drumming by masked dancers.

Hire a car or bicycle. 2 hours by bus; 2½ hours by train from Kanazawa via Wajima.

Obuse

For lovers of *ukiyo-e* woodblock prints and devotees of the master artist Hokusai, Obuse is worth a visit. When Hokusai was an old man, one of the merchants here became his patron and Obuse has a museum with a fine collection of some of his best late works – depictions of elephants, tigers, *ukiyo-e* beauties and Mount Fuji with a dragon issuing from its mouth.

20 minutes from Nagano by train. Hokusai-kan (Hokusai Museum). Tel: 026 247 5206. Open: Apr–Oct daily 9am–5pm; 9.30am–4.30pm in winter. Admission charge.

Osaka

According to Japanese lore, when Osakans meet they don't ask: 'How are you?' but rather 'Making any money?' Founded by the great warlord Toyotomi Hideyoshi in the 16th century, Osaka was and is a city of merchants. Today it is Japan's third-largest city. Much of the country's industrial output is produced here, including textiles, pharmaceuticals, iron and steel, and 40 per cent of exports pass through Osaka's airport and docks. Osaka used to be a city of concrete, but in recent years it has become more pleasant: trees line its boulevards and parks are being laid out. There are a few historical sights, notably Hideyoshi's fortress, **Osaka Castle**, once a fortified city. The present castle is a reconstruction, but still worth seeing. **Sumiyoshi Shrine** in the south of the city,

founded in the 4th or 5th century, has a beautiful arched bridge. **Shitennoji** was founded in 593; only Asuka Temple (*see p123*) is older.

However, the essence of Osaka is not in its past but in its bustling streets, dazzling neon nightscapes and extraordinary modern architecture. The north of the city, centring around Osaka station, is more refined. Here, look out for the new **Shin-Umeda Building**, in a complex that includes the glamorous Westin Hotel. The building has observation galleries on the roof and top floor, reached by a glass lift. As you move south, the lights grow brighter and the designs wilder. Be sure not to miss the Shinsaibashi/Dotombori area by night, where giant crabs, lobsters and dragons wave claws along the neon-lit streets, and the wonderful glowing white, futuristic towers of Kirin Plaza on Ebisu Bridge resemble a surreal lantern. Forget good and bad taste and enjoy the Japanese at play.

The **Kaiyukan Aquarium** in the Tempozan area is one of the largest in the world and worth a visit.

45 minutes from Kansai International Airport; 2½ hours from Tokyo by train. Osaka Tourist Information Centre. Tel: 06 6305 3311.

There is a Tourist Information Centre at Osaka and Shin-Osaka stations, Osaka airport and also at Kansai International Airport.

www.tourism.city.osaka.jp

Traditional farmhouses in Shirakawa

Shirakawa and Gokayama

In the narrow valleys between the mountains of central Japan, the villagers of Shirakawa and Gokayama built *gassho-zukuri* houses. These enormous wooden farmhouses have huge smoke-darkened rafters and steeply sloping thatched roofs, like two hands pressed together in prayer (*gassho*). Many are now inns where visitors can experience the lifestyle of these country areas. In Shirakawa there is a folkcraft museum, a temple and fine mountain views. The villages of Gokayama are scattered along a spectacular gorge; the prettiest is Ainokura, nearest to Kanazawa.

2½ hours north of Takayama; 2 hours from Kanazawa by infrequent bus.

Takayama

Surrounded by spectacular mountain ranges and in the past often cut off by snow, Takayama developed a robust and distinctive culture. Visitors come to stroll through the streets of splendid wooden houses, buy Takayama's woodcrafts and taste the mountain cuisine. The Takayama Festival (Sanno Matsuri), held in April, is well worth attending. If you plan to stay in Takayama during the festival, it is advisable to book accommodation well in advance. The best way to explore the town is by bicycle.

Asa-ichi (Morning Market)

In the morning, farmers bring vegetables, *miso* (soybean paste) and handicrafts and spread them along the riverside to sell. It's a lively scene, and you can indulge in some haggling.

Hida Minzoku Mura (Hida Folk Village)

Hida Folk Village is full of the nostalgic smell of woodsmoke. This famous open-air museum consists of 30 of the finest old farmhouses from the mountains around Takayama, lovingly reassembled. The buildings, of smoke-blackened wood with huge beams and thickly thatched roofs, were made in the traditional way, without nails.

5 minutes by bus south of station.
Tel: 0577 33 4711.
Open: daily 8.30am–5pm.
Admission charge.

Kusakabe Mingeikan (Kusakabe Folk Museum)

This splendid house was built by the Kusakabe family in 1879 when, after years of repression, merchants were finally able to display their wealth. Made of the finest timbers, it is striking for its sheer size and lofty ceilings criss-crossed by enormous beams. Next door is **Yoshijima-ke** (Yoshijima house), an elegant merchant's house of 1908.

20-minute walk north of station.
Open: Apr–Nov daily 8.30am–5pm (till 4.30pm in winter).
Yoshijima-ke. Open: Mar–Nov Wed–Mon 9am–4.30pm. Admission charge to each.

San-machi Suji (San-machi Street)

San-machi Suji is the merchants' quarter and the heart of the old town.

The narrow streets are lined with picturesque shops, restaurants, inns and sake breweries, the last marked by a ball of cryptomeria leaves.

Across the red bridge from Takayama Jinya.

Takayama Jinya
(Takayama Government Office)
Built as the palace of the local daimyo in 1615, this splendid building was taken over by the officers of the shogun in 1692 to use as the provincial government offices. There is a memorable torture chamber with instruments of torture and vivid depictions of how they were used. Next to the main building is an enormous storehouse, the oldest extant, where sacks of rice, sent as taxes to the shogun, were stored.

10-minute walk from station.
Open: Apr–Oct daily 8.45am–5pm (till 4.30pm in winter). Admission charge.

Takayama is 2¼ hours north of Nagoya by train. Tourist information office and bicycle rental at station.

Toba
Toba is the home of **Pearl Island**, where Kokichi Mikimoto first succeeded in producing a cultured pearl. There is a pearl museum here, and you can also watch *ama*, women divers who dive supposedly for pearls (in fact they are diving for shellfish and seaweed). The surrounding area is very picturesque.

15 minutes east of Ise; 1¾ hours south of Nagoya by train.

There are many types of *Jizo* statues throughout Japan to protect children

Yoshino
This mountain, deep in the heart of the central Japanese peninsula, has long been a place of retreat. Mountain priests carried out ascetic practices and emperors and lords fled here from their enemies. Today Yoshino is famous for its cherry blossom. In April the entire mountain is carpeted with pale pink blossom and the narrow village street is jam-packed. For the rest of the year it is quiet. People come to visit the temple of **Kimpusenji** and to climb through the village to the mountaintop shrine of **Kimpu-jinja**.

1¼ hours south of Osaka by train, then cable car.
Kimpusenji. Open: daily 9am–5pm. Free admission.
Kimpu-jinja. Always open. Free admission.

Walk: The Nakasendo 'Mountain Road'

This 7km (4-mile) hike takes you along a section of the old Nakasendo Highway, which used to run from Kyoto to Tokyo, through the mountain country of central Japan.

Allow 4 hours.

From Nakatsugawa, 1 hour northeast of Nagoya by train, take a bus to Magome (35 minutes).

1 Magome

Magome is a picturesque little town which straggles steeply up the hill along the old Nakasendo Highway. Post towns, which sprang up along highways to cater to travellers, were always long and narrow, lining the street on both sides with inns, restaurants, tearooms and pleasure houses. Magome is one of the very few post towns to remain much as it was. The shuttered wooden buildings, waterwheels and cobbled streets have been carefully preserved. There are few electric cables visible and no cars, though souvenir shops have now replaced pleasure houses. As you climb the hill you will pass a museum dedicated to the town's most famous son, the novelist Shimazaki Toson (1872–1943).

Shimazaki Toson Museum. Open: Fri–Mon 8am–5pm. Admission charge.

At the road, walk or take a bus to Magome Pass. The path is clear and well signposted. Look for signs to Tsumago-juku in English.

2 Magome-Toge (Magome Pass)

At Magome Pass, 801m (2,628ft) above
sea level, there is a teashop and views
across the surrounding mountains.
From here, take the stony path which
leads to the right of the teahouse steeply
down into forest. At the time of the
shoguns, there were only two highways
linking Tokyo and Kyoto: the Tokaido,
which went along the coast, skirting
Mount Fuji, and the Nakasendo. People
walked or travelled by palanquin or on
horseback; wheeled traffic was
forbidden. Along the way you pass a
checkpoint, where guards were posted
to prevent timber smuggling.
*Follow the path out of the forest through
a small village to a bridge. On the other
side is the village of Otsumago.*

Pretty mountain views along the Nakasendo
Highway

3 Otsumago

Otsumago's handsome old farmhouses
still provide accommodation to passing
travellers. Even if you don't stay, you
can admire the dark wooden shutters
and heavy overhanging eaves. There is
also a working waterwheel.
*Follow the path downhill to Tsumago.
From Magome Pass the walk takes
about 2 hours.*

4 Tsumago

Tsumago is the most picturesque and
perfectly preserved of the old post
towns. You can stroll the cobbled
streets, stay in one of the romantic old
inns which have welcomed travellers for
centuries, and try mountain vegetables,
soba buckwheat noodles and *gohei*

mochi – rice cakes threaded on skewers
and dressed with a nutty paste. The
street is lined with dark wooden houses,
pressed close together, with shop signs
hanging outside; many sell local
handicrafts. There is also an
atmospheric old shrine, the village
temple (up some stone steps), and the
house of the village magnate, made of
hinoki (cypress), now a folk museum
(Okuya Kyodokan).
*Okuya Kyodokan. Tel: 0264 57 3322.
Open: daily 9am–4.45pm.
Admission charge.
From Tsumago, the Nakasendo winds off
invitingly to Nagiso, where you can take
a train to Nagoya or Matsumoto. The
walk takes 2 hours. Alternatively, you can
take a bus, which takes 7 minutes.*

By bike: The Asuka Plain

This cycle ride traces the earliest Japanese civilisation, taking you through bamboo groves, rolling hills and paddy fields.

Allow 3–4 hours.

Take the train to Asuka, 1 hour south of Nara, via Kashihara-jingu-mae; also accessible from Osaka and Kyoto. At Asuka station, hire a bicycle. Cross the main road and follow the cycling track off to your left; watch for signposts in English to Takamatsuzaka tumulus.

1 Takamatsuzaka Kofun (Takamatsuzaka Tumulus)

The ride from Asuka station takes you through a serene, ageless landscape. Tucked into the hillside is the **Takamatsuzaka Barrow Mural Museum**; the tumulus itself is a few steps further on. When the tumulus was excavated in 1972, archaeologists found a chamber painted with astonishingly delicate and beautiful 7th-century frescoes akin to Tang Chinese painting. These depicted people in court costume, a dragon, a tiger and a tortoise with a snake coiled around it. The tumulus is now sealed to preserve the frescoes, but you can see perfect full-scale reproductions in the museum.

Takamatsuzaka Barrow Mural Museum. Tel: 0744 54 3340. Open: Tue–Sun 9am–5pm. Admission charge.
Return to the main road; take the cycling path which runs beside it. Watch for signposts in English for Ishibutai.

2 Ishibutai

To your left you pass a large tumulus, the mausoleum of Emperor Temmu and Empress Jito. Cycle on and look for signs to Kameishi, an enormous rock carved with the face of a tortoise. On your right you pass **Tachibana Temple**, said to be the birthplace of Prince Shotoku (*see pp113–14*). Finally, at the top of a long incline, you come to Ishibutai ('Stone Stage'), an enormous 7th-century barrow, surrounded by a dry moat and roofed with flat stones.

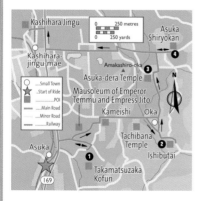

Asuka Tourist Information Office
Tel: 0744 54 2001.

*Ishibutai Barrow. Open: Tue–Sun
9am–5pm. Admission charge.*
*Cycle back down the hill and follow signs
to Asuka-dera Temple; or study the maps
that dot the area and take one of the
cycling paths that wind through the hills
to the temple.*

3 Asuka-dera Temple

Asuka-dera Temple houses the oldest
bronze Buddha in Japan, a large, serene
image dating from 607. It has been
through many fires and only the face
and hands are original. The temple was
founded in 588 and is the oldest in
Japan. Behind it is a small stone pagoda.
*Open: Apr–Sept daily 8am–5.30pm
(till 5pm in winter). Admission
charge.*
*Turn left out of the temple. At the main
road turn right to Asuka Museum.*

4 Asuka Shiryokan (Asuka Museum)

In the garden is a fountain made of two
grotesque embracing figures,
representative of the many strange
stone figures which dot the area. Inside
is a detailed exhibition of the many
discoveries that have cast light on the
highly advanced culture which
developed in this area in the 7th
century. Look in particular at the water-
clock, perpetually filling and emptying
to indicate the passage of time. The
exhibition is being continually updated
as recent excavations reveal new
information.
*Open: Tue–Sun 9am–4.30pm.
Admission charge.*
*Cycle back down the hill to Kashihara
Jingu (Kashihara Shrine), dedicated to
Japan's first emperor, Jimmu. Return
your bicycle at Kashihara-jingu-mae
station, from where there are trains to
Osaka, Kyoto and Nara.*

Asuka-dera Temple, Japan's first true Buddhist temple

Western Honshu and Shikoku

Western Japan is an area of contrasts – mountains and sea, shadows and light. At its heart is the Setonaikai (Seto Inland Sea), bounded by Honshu to the north and Shikoku to the south. Islands dot the sparkling water and boats ply to and fro. Ancient battles took place here, and from these shores envoys once sailed back and forth between Japan and mainland Asia.

North of the sea is San-yo ('the Sunny Side of the Mountains'), bustling with life and action. The bullet train runs along the coast and there is much heavy industry. But across the mountain ranges in San-in ('in the Shadow of the Mountains'), along the Sea of Japan coast, life moves at a slower pace. The weather – cool and rainy – reflects the mood of this rural backwater.

Shikoku, the smallest of Japan's four main islands, is more remote still.

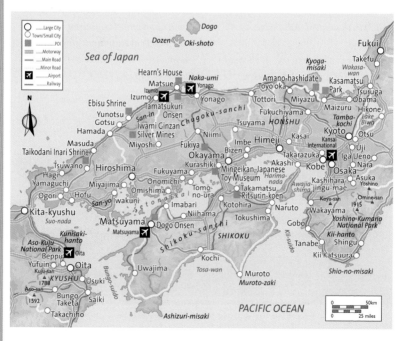

Along the Inland Sea coast are busy ports. But travel inland and you find yourself among tangerine groves, terraced paddy fields and forested mountains, little changed over hundreds of years. Every year many people make the pilgrimage around Shikoku's 88 temples, circling the island in the footsteps of Japan's greatest saint, Kobo Daishi (774–835), who was born here. Today, Shikoku is more accessible than ever before, linked to the mainland by the **Seto-Ohashi Bridge**, which carries road and rail traffic.

Amano-hashidate

This delicate sandspit, which is covered in gnarled pines, stretches across Miyazu Bay like the 'bridge of heaven' that is the meaning of its name, and is traditionally considered to be one of Japan's most beautiful sights.

The recommended way to look at it is from **Kasamatsu Park**, on the other side of the bay, where you are supposed to bend over and admire the view from between your legs (from this rather ungainly position Amano-hashidate is said to appear as if floating in mid-air).
San-in, 2 hours northwest of Kyoto by train.

Bizen

The most sought-after pottery in Japan is Bizen ware, handmade with local clay and baked in wood-fired climbing kilns (many-chambered clay kilns built up the side of a hill). The pine ash used for firing gives a natural glaze to the ware.

In the village of **Imbe**, near Bizen city, and the surrounding area, many ceramics museums can be found. The best one is **Kibi-do**.
San-yo, 40 minutes east of Okayama by train (Imbe station).
Kibi-do (Ceramics Museum). Imbe. Tel: 0869 64 4467. Open: Tue–Sun 10am–6pm. Admission charge.

Fukiya

Situated in some of the most beautiful mountain country in Japan, Fukiya was a prosperous community a hundred years ago, producing copper and red ochre (used to stain woodwork). Wealthy mine-owners commissioned splendid houses before the copper ran out and Fukiya turned into a ghost town. Today, the old houses are being restored and you can visit the ochre mill and copper mine.
San-yo, 2 hours northwest of Kurashiki, by train and infrequent bus.

Dawn breaks over a glorious beach at the old fishing port of Hagi

The Atomic Bomb Dome stands by the Aioi River in Hiroshima

Hagi

This gracious old fishing port is famous for its lustrous rose-coloured pottery and romantic history.

From 1600 onwards Hagi was the domain of the Mori lords, opponents of the shogun. In 1868, when the shoguns were overthrown, fiery young men from Hagi were at the forefront of the rebellion. Japanese visitors still come to pay their respects at the birthplaces and graves of these heroes, and to wander through the streets of samurai houses.

San-in, 2 hours from Kokura (Kita-kyushu) by train; 1½ hours by express bus from Ogori bullet train station.

Himeji

Its white turrets soaring above the plain like some great bird, Himeji Castle –

'the White Egret' – is one of the few remaining originals as opposed to the concrete reconstructions normally seen. Built in 1580, it is indisputably Japan's most spectacular castle. Until the Meiji Restoration, it was a living, working castle, home to a succession of feudal lords and their innumerable retainers. You can climb the zigzag path to the castle entrance, its convoluted course providing the defenders with ample opportunity to bombard you from the many openings in the castle walls. If you have time for only one Japanese castle, this should be it.

San-yo, 30 minutes west of Osaka by train.

Hiroshima

Hiroshima would be no more than a large industrial city, with no particular interest, but for the dreadful event of 6 August 1945 when it was the target for the world's first atomic bomb. The city has been rebuilt, but the A-Bomb Dome and Peace Park are eternal memorials.

Genbaku Domu (Atomic Bomb Dome)

The Industrial Promotion Hall was almost exactly at the epicentre of the explosion. Its skeletal ruin is now the city's symbol.

Heiwa Kinen Koen
(Peace Memorial Park)

The Peace Park contains memorials to the victims of the atomic bomb and there is also an eternal flame (to be extinguished when the last nuclear weapon has been destroyed). The Peace Memorial Museum in the park is a stark collection of items – the shadow of a man who had been standing outside a bank, watches fused at 8.15 – all the more moving for the simplicity of the presentation. A new wing explains the USA's decision to drop the bomb.
Park and museum. Open: May–Nov daily 8.30am–6pm (till 5pm in winter). www.pcf.city.hiroshima.jp.
Admission charge.

San-yo, 4 hours west of Tokyo by bullet train. Information offices in station and Peace Memorial Park.

Himeji Castle dates from the 16th century

Izumo

At the foot of steep, forested hills, in a magnificent natural setting, is Japan's oldest Shinto shrine, Izumo Taisha, dedicated to Okuninushi, deity of good fortune and marriage. Worshippers invoke Okuninushi by clapping four times.

San-in, 30 minutes west of Matsue by train and bus; also accessible by plane. Shrine always open. Free admission.

Kochi

Cut off from the northern coast of Shikoku by near-impenetrable mountain ranges, the charming old city of Kochi has a Mediterranean flavour, with palm-lined streets, hot-blooded locals and a noisy morning market. It is famous for its fighting dogs, the Tosa

A child greets a statue of a dog in Kotohira Shrine

LAFCADIO HEARN (1850–1904)

The English writer Lafcadio Hearn arrived in Matsue in 1890 and spent the rest of his life in Japan. He married a local girl and lived and dressed as a Japanese. He also took a Japanese name, Yakumo Koizumi, and became a naturalised Japanese citizen.

From Matsue he moved to Kobe and later to Tokyo, but Matsue remained his first love. In his books, of which *Glimpses of Unfamiliar Japan* is the best known, he wrote of Japan and Japanese culture in page after page of purple prose. After his death he was honoured for his services to Japan.

mastiffs, who are ranked like sumo wrestlers. Kochi Castle, rebuilt in 1753, was more of a residence than a castle, impossible to defend, having living quarters on the ground floor opening on to the garden.

Shikoku, 2½ hours south of Okayama by train; also accessible by plane.
Castle. Open: daily 9am–5pm (last entry 4.30pm). Admission charge.

Kotohira

One of the best-loved pilgrimage places in Japan, Kotohira Shrine (1837) sprawls spectacularly across a mountainside. The main shrine is 800 steps up, in easy stages, with palanquins for the old or faint-hearted. Dedicated to the sun goddess Ama-terasu, it is a wonderful, weatherbeaten building, ornately carved and thatch-roofed, with long verandas looking towards the Shikoku hills and across to the Inland Sea. The shrine is particularly venerated by seafarers, who have left offerings of model ships and old photographs of steamers.

Shikoku, 30 minutes southwest of Takamatsu; 1 hour south of Okayama by train.

Kurashiki

In feudal times Kurashiki's excellent rice was stored in whitewashed warehouses (*kura* means 'warehouse'), one of which was later used by industrialist local-boy-made-good Keisaburo Ohara to display his collection of Western art.

Today, Kurashiki is famous for its museums, and the canal area, lined with old warehouses and willows, is a preservation zone.

Besides the Ohara Museum, you can see the **Mingeikan** (Folk Art Museum), the **Japanese Toy Museum**, and many others.

San-yo, 15 minutes west of Okayama by train. Museums open: Tue–Sun 8am–5pm. Admission charge for each.

MOMOTARO

The legend of Momotaro is famous in Okayama prefecture. An old woman found a giant peach floating in the water of the nearby river and she took it home to her husband to eat. When she cut it open, however, there was a small boy inside. She and her husband named him Momotaro, or 'Peach Boy', and raised him to be big and strong. One day Momotaro went off to Ogre Island with his friends the monkey, the pheasant and the dog, and between them they defeated the evil ogres, returning to his home in Okayama with the treasure.

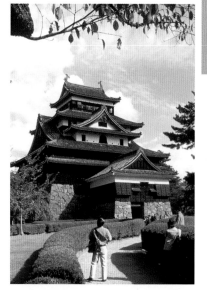

Matsue Castle, in the city beloved of Lafcadio Hearn and now a magnet for his admirers

Matsue

Lafcadio Hearn (*see box opposite*) dubbed Matsue 'The Chief City of the Province of the Gods' and immortalised it in his books. Today, **Hearn's house** has become a place of pilgrimage for his many Japanese readers. Matsue's black 17th-century **castle** is the city's other attraction, 'a vast and sinister shape, all iron-grey, rising against the sky from a cyclopean foundation of stone . . .', as Hearn described it.

San-in, 2½ hours northwest of Okayama by train; or take a flight to Izumo or Yonago airport.

Koizumi Yakumo Kyukyo (Lafcadio Hearn's house). Tel: 0852 23 0714. Open: daily 9am–4.40pm. Admission charge.

The charm of Okayama Castle

Matsue Castle. Tel: 0852 21 4030.
Open: daily 8.30am–6pm (till 4.30pm in
winter). Admission charge.

Matsuyama

High on a hill above the noise and
bustle of the city, **Matsuyama Castle**
with its turrets, donjon and massive
stone walls evokes the samurai age.
It competes for tourists' attention with
Dogo Onsen, whose thermal waters are
famous for helping stiff joints,
digestion and nerves.

1 hour by hydrofoil from Hiroshima;
2¾ hours from Okayama by train; also
acccessible by plane.
Castle. 10 minutes from station by tram.
Tel: 089 921 4873. Open: daily
9am–5pm. Admission charge.
Dogo Onsen. 20 minutes from station by
tram. Open: daily 6.30am–11pm.
Admission charge.

Miyajima

Despite being one of the most famous
places in Japan, Miyajima is truly
magical. Visit in the evening and you
have the place to yourself (along with the
tame deer that roam the streets).
Miyajima ('Shrine Island') was once so
sacred that laypeople were not permitted
to step on its soil but approached by
boat, via the huge *torii* which seems to
float on the water at high tide. Wander
round the island, explore the pagodas
and temples, or ascend Mount Misen
(on foot or by cable car) for a spectacular
view over the Inland Sea.
San-yo, by train to Miyajima-guchi,
15 minutes west of Hiroshima, then ferry.

Okayama

Okayama is a large city with several
museums, a charming castle, and a
garden officially rated one of Japan's
three most beautiful. **Okayama Castle**
(1597, but reconstructed after World
War II), nicknamed 'Crow Castle', is
pitch-black. **Korakuen** is a perfect
Japanese garden, a world in miniature,
with hills, lakes, pavilions, even paddy
fields and a tea plantation.

*San-yo, 50 minutes west of Osaka by
train; also accessible by plane.
Castle. 5 minutes east of station by tram.
Tel: 086 225 2096. Open: daily
9am–5pm. Admission charge.
Korakuen. Beside castle. Tel: 086 272
1148. Open: Apr–Sept daily
7.30am–6pm; 8am–5pm in winter.
Admission charge.*

Takamatsu

This lively port city at the southern end
of Seto-Ohashi Bridge is the main
gateway to Shikoku from Honshu. Its
chief glory is **Ritsurin-koen** (Ritsurin
Park), with manicured pine trees and
lakes full of carp.
*Ritsurin-koen. 10 minutes by train south
of station. Open: daily dawn–dusk.
Admission charge.*

Tomo-no-ura

On their way to Edo (Tokyo) to pay
respects to the shoguns, Korean
emissaries used to stay at Taichi-ro, the
Wave-facing Pavilion, in Tomo-no-ura.
The view from there, they declared, was
the loveliest in Japan. Not only the view
– like an ink-brush painting – but the
whole of this picturesque fishing port is
a delight. Roam the narrow lanes,
explore the castle ruins, or take a ferry
out to the beaches on the islands.
*San-yo, 30 minutes south by bus from
Fukuyama station.*

Tsuwano

This pretty country town lies in a valley
with steep hills rising to either side.

High on one hillside are the ornate
orange buildings of **Taikodani Inari
Shrine**, reached through a tunnel of
2,000 *torii* or along a road blazoned
with red banners. The ruins of Tsuwano
Castle lie at the top of the ridge.
*San-in, near Hagi, 1 hour by train from
Ogori bullet train station; 2 hours by
steam train on summer Sundays (book
in advance).*

Yunotsu

Yunotsu is a charming port town in
Shimane. Both Yunotsu and the nearby
Iwami Ginzan Silver Mines were
registered as a UNESCO World Heritage
Site in July 2007. The 600 silver mine
shafts and some of the temples date
back to the 14th century. The **Ebisu
Shrine**, in particular, was built in 1526
and is one of the oldest shrines in
Japan. Yunotsu is also home to one of
the best *onsen* in Japan: **Yakushiyu**,
which is one of only 13 facilities in
Japan to be awarded the highest grade
by the Japanese Hot Spring Association.
Don't miss **Shinyu Café**, in an old
heritage-listed bathhouse.
*Iwami Ginzan Silver Mines. A bus
service departs from Hiroshima train
station and Hiroshima Bus Centre twice
a day to Ohda City and the Iwami
Ginzan Silver Mines. Tel: 0854 82 0662.
Ebisu Shrine. At port entrance.
Yakushiyu. Tel: 0855 65 4894. Open:
daily 5am–9pm. Admission charge.
Shinyu Café. Tel: 0855 65 4126.
Open: Fri–Wed 11am–5pm.
www.yunotsu.com*

Cruise: The Inland Sea

The Inland Sea (Setonaikai), with its misty islands rising from clear blue waters, is one of the most beautiful places in Japan. It has its quota of industries, particularly on the Honshu side, but you can still enjoy the unhurried pace of life on the islands.

Day trip.

The easiest and most popular way to see the islands is aboard a Setonaikai (SKK) cruise, which goes from Miyajima to Onomichi, not far from Kurashiki (reduced services in winter). To book your ticket beforehand tel: 082 253 1212. www.setonaikaikisen.co.jp. Alternatively, use ferries to hop from island to island – tourist information centres can suggest several options. Start from Miyajima or Hiroshima and buy a ticket initially for Omishima.

1 Miyajima

The most enchanting place to begin your journey is at the ancient holy island of Miyajima (*see p130*), one of the great sights of Japan.

You set off, leaving its huge red *torii* behind you. There are said to be 3,000 islands in the Setonaikai (Inland Sea), most crowded into the stretch of water you are about to go through, and many have names and stories connected with them. Fishing boats and barges ply

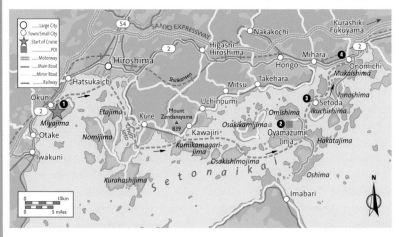

between fishing villages, past tiny craggy islands.

Pass through Ondo Straits, said to have been dug out by the warlord Kiyomori Taira 800 years ago, and through a succession of small islands to reach Omishima.

2 Omishima

Omishima is famous for its shrine, **Oyamazumi Jinja**, where the pirates who once controlled the Inland Sea used to worship. The shrine also has a treasure house full of armour and weapons which belonged to great heroes from Japanese history. But rather than seeing these you may prefer to use the two-hour break in your tour to borrow a bicycle (rent free, at the pier). Cycle around the island on the well-marked cycling paths and savour the empty roads, orange groves, slate-roofed cottages and rugged forested hills.

From Omishima take the boat or a ferry to Setoda, the port on Ikuchishima island.

3 Setoda

The tourist attraction here is **Kosanji**, a bizarre construction erected by a local who made his fortune in the steel tube industry, and dedicated the temple to his mother. You may safely avoid this. Instead, rent a bicycle at the pier and spend your free hour exploring the island. The port town of Setoda itself is full of charming old houses. Inland there is a large lake formed by a dam

Miyajima's majestic *torii* is the first of many remarkable views along the Inland Sea cruise

Cruise: The Inland Sea

from where you can look back to the bay, full of cranes and fishing boats, and to the islands all around.

From Setoda, take the boat or a ferry on to Onomichi.

4 Onomichi

Onomichi, back on the Honshu mainland, is an interesting little town straggling a hillside and overlooked by a tiny castle. Most of the streets are too steep and narrow for cars. Walk along the lanes, exploring the innumerable temples: the most notable are **Senkoji**, at the top of the hill, and **Jodoji**, which has a long history and some unusual buildings.

From Onomichi, the JR Sanyo Line has trains every 15 minutes east to Fukuyama, for Tomo-no-ura (see p131), Okayama or Osaka, or west to Hiroshima.

The tropical south

If you are travelling by bullet train, your first view of Kyushu, the southernmost of Japan's four main islands, will be the smokestacks and shipyards of Kita-kyushu. Kyushu has been dubbed Japan's Silicon Island; besides being home to the massive Nippon Steel Works, Kita-kyushu is the country's centre for the manufacture of semiconductors and IC chips.

Don't worry. Once clear of the northernmost strip, the south of Japan is idyllically beautiful. Japanese holiday-makers visit Kyushu for its panoramic views and dramatic live volcanoes. This is where the history of Japan, both legendary and factual, begins. It is said that when the wind god Ninigi came to rule Japan, he alighted on Mount Takachiho in the Kirishima range. And it seems likely that remote ancestors of the Japanese, among them the ancestors of the Imperial family, migrated from Korea, on mainland Asia, across to Kyushu.

Okinawa, with its clear blue seas and silver beaches, is a paradise for watersports, with the best scuba diving in Asia. The people and culture are completely distinct from Japanese, and there are many traces of that ancient culture to be found.

TAKAMORI SAIGO (1827–77)

The great romantic hero of Japan's modern era was Takamori Saigo, a larger-than-life figure, with eyes that sparkled 'like black diamonds' and a great bull head. A poor samurai from the southern city of Kagoshima, he was a brilliant soldier, instrumental in the overthrow of the shogun and the Meiji Restoration of 1868. He became part of the new government, but on finding himself opposed to his colleagues, retreated to Kagoshima, from where, in 1877, he launched a rebellion which failed. On 23 September Saigo committed ritual suicide.

Aso-Kuju National Park

Fifty thousand years ago, a series of huge explosions produced one of the largest calderas on earth. Within Mount Aso's vast outer rim, more than 20km (12 miles) across, are farms, villages and several smaller volcanoes. One at least is far from dormant. You can take the cable car or drive to the rim of Naka-dake and peer at the seething green lava in its depths.

It is worth stopping off at the nearby town of **Bungo Taketa** to admire the romantic ruins of **Oka Castle**, perched high on the ridge.

The tropical south

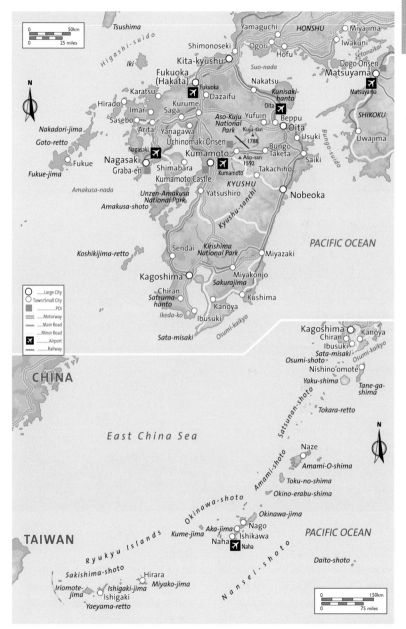

Mount Aso in Aso-Kuju National Park

Central Kyushu, 1 hour east of
Kumamoto; 2 hours southwest of Beppu
by train. Bus from station to cable car.
Bungo Taketa lies between Aso and
Beppu by train or bus.

Beppu

Beppu is a large seaside city whose
major industry is fun. It is crammed
with hotels, neon signs, tour buses
and a breathtaking variety of

entertainments. For hot-spring enthusiasts Beppu is paradise. There are 'hells', where steam and hot water gush from the rocks, and many different spas – outdoor pools, jungle baths and hot sands. There is even a sex museum. If nothing else, Beppu does provide an insight into the Japanese at play.
Northeast Kyushu, accessible by plane (Oita airport). 2½ hours southeast of Hakata; 3½ hours northeast of Kumamoto by train.

Dazaifu

Once the ancient capital of Kyushu and southern outpost of the Nara government, Dazaifu is a place of pilgrimage for millions of students eager to pass their exams. Just beyond the station, shops selling calligraphy brushes line the entrance to **Tenman-gu Shrine**, dedicated to Tenjin, god of poets and calligraphers. A historical figure, Tenjin was a 9th-century scholar named Sugawara-no Michizane, who was exiled to Dazaifu and died there. Besides his shrine, the small town of Dazaifu has several important temples.
Northern Kyushu, 20 minutes southeast of Fukuoka by train.

Fukuoka

Step off the bullet train at Fukuoka, and you could be in Tokyo. Fukuoka (confusingly, the station is called Hakata, after the old merchant quarter, while the city is called Fukuoka, after the samurai section) is no backwoods provincial city. It's known as Japan's

shopping capital, and in 2009 *Monocle* magazine rated it the world's 16th most livable city.

Fukuoka has its quota of historical sights, notably the 12th-century **Shofukuji**, Japan's oldest Zen temple. But primarily it is a sparkling modern city. The Tenjin area is where the young and chic go shopping; to see affluent modern Japan, visit the gold-plated IMS Building there. The Nakasu area, between Fukuoka's two rivers, comes alive in the evening, when everyone goes to eat, drink and be merry. Fukuoka also boasts the largest seaside tower in Japan – the 234m (768ft) high **Fukuoka Tower**, incorporating 8,000 mirrors – and the country's most hi-tech baseball stadium. The Fukuoka Dome is also here. It opened in 1993 and is home to the city's proudest acquisition, the Daiei Hawks baseball team.
Northern Kyushu, 6½ hours west of Tokyo by train; also accessible by plane.

Kagoshima

Even on fine days there is always a faint pall of smoke over Kagoshima. Wherever you turn, you can't fail to notice the brooding cone of the volcano Sakurajima across the bay, trailing an ominous plume of smoke. Often umbrellas are up, as a drizzle of black ash rains down on the city.

For centuries the capital of the Shimazu clan, Kagoshima has a long, idiosyncratic history. St Francis Xavier landed here in 1549, determined to convert Japan to Christianity, while in the 19th century the fiery Shimazu clan led the rebellion to topple the shogun. Modern Kagoshima is a port and industrial city.

Iso Teien (Iso Garden)

The Shimazu lords built their villa against the spectacular backdrop of Sakurajima. You can stroll through the rooms, lined with gold leaf, where they entertained Western potentates. In the grounds is a fascinating historical museum in Japan's first modern factory, which was established by the Shimazu.

10 minutes north of Kagoshima station by bus. Tel: 099 247 1551. Open: Mar–Oct daily 8.30am–5.30pm (till 5pm in winter). Admission charge.

Sakurajima

The most exciting thing to do in Kagoshima is to take the ferry across to Sakurajima, which means 'cherry blossom island' though this is an extremely lively volcano and has small eruptions every day. One huge explosion in 1914 produced enough lava to join the island to the mainland, while another buried several villages. The most recent big eruption was in 1960. There are several lookout points around the island, with breathtaking views, and lava shelters in case of another eruption.

15 minutes from Sakurajima Pier by ferry, ferries operate 24 hours. There are buses around the volcano, or hire a bicycle.

Kagoshima is in southern Kyushu, 4 hours south of Hakata by train; also accessible by plane. Tourist information: Nishi-Kagoshima station. Tel: 099 253 2500.

Kagoshima environs

Kagoshima is the gateway to the Satsuma-hanto (Satsuma Peninsula) and some of Japan's most glorious tropical scenery. The journey down the coast takes you past white beaches, rocky outcrops, dense bamboo groves and hillsides covered in tea plantations or terraced paddy fields. At the tip of the peninsula is Lake Ikeda, a serene caldera lake where giant eels reside. The picture-book-perfect cone of Mount Kaimon is also located here.

Chiran

In this charming small town, a whole street of samurai houses is preserved. Each has a garden using rocks, stone lanterns, hedges and raked gravel to create a landscape in miniature.

Chiran was one of the bases from which the kamikaze pilots took off in the last desperate months of World War II. The **Tokko Heiwa Kaikan** (Peace Museum for Kamikaze Pilots) is a collection of memorabilia – letters, photographs, aeroplanes – of the youths who died.

1¼ hours by bus south of Kagoshima. Samurai street. Open: daily 8am–5.30pm. Admission charge. Tokko Heiwa Kaikan. Tel: 099 383 2525. Open: daily 9am–5pm. Admission charge.

Ibusuki

A pleasant seaside town, Ibusuki offers two extraordinary experiences. One is being buried up to your neck in steaming hot sand. The other is the **Jungle Bath**, where you bathe in a variety of pools surrounded by tropical foliage. There is also a museum of modern art, the **Iwasaki Bijutsukan**, in a building designed by one of Japan's leading architects, Fumihiko Maki.

1 hour south of Kagoshima by train. Sunamushi-buro (sand bath), on the beach, is a 20-minute walk from station. Open: daily 8.30am–8.30pm. Jungle Bath, in Kanko Hotel. Open: daily 7am–10pm.

Iwasaki Bijutsukan, next to Kanko Hotel. Open: daily 8am–5.30pm. Admission charge to all.

Kirishima National Park

The peaks of the Kirishima range rise out of lush tropical countryside. According to ancient creation myths, this is where the wind god Ninigi alighted when he came down to rule earth. His halberd is still there, embedded on the top of Mount Takachiho. A spectacular day-long walk will take you across five peaks to Takachiho's vast bowl-shaped crater.

Southern Kyushu, 2 hours by train and bus north of Kagoshima.

The smoking cone of Sakurajima, seen from the ferry on its way back to Kagoshima

Kumamoto

Kumamoto is a large, energetic, modern city, with NEC, the world's largest producer of microchips, as its main employer. The city's magnificent **castle** burnt down in 1877 while under siege by Takamori Saigo (*see box on p134*). It was rebuilt and houses a fascinating collection of treasures of the Hosokawa clan, the long-time rulers of the area.

Kumamoto's elaborate landscaped garden, **Suizenji Koen** (Suizenji Park), features a miniature Mount Fuji covered in grass as the focal point of interest. *Western Kyushu, accessible by plane; 1½ hours south of Fukuoka by train. Kumamoto Castle, 15 minutes by tram from station. Open: Apr–Oct daily 8.30am–5.30pm (till 4.30pm in winter). Admission charge.*

A corner turret of Kumamoto's massive castle, rebuilt after the original was destroyed by fire

Suizenji Park, 30 minutes by tram from station. Open: Mar–Nov daily 7.30am–6pm; 8.30am–5pm in winter. Admission charge.

Kunisaki-hanto (Kunisaki Peninsula)

One of the most isolated and remote corners of Japan, Kunisaki has steep wooded hills, with tiny villages tucked into the valleys or high on the hillsides. A Buddhist stronghold in ancient times, it is rich in stone images and ancient temples.

Northeastern Kyushu, accessible by plane (Oita airport); car or bus tour from Beppu.

Nagasaki

Nagasaki hit world headlines on 9 August 1945, when the second atomic bomb laid it waste and ended World War II. Before that this picturesque port city, straggling up the hillsides around Nagasaki Bay, had a long history of contact with the West, and its streets and old buildings tell the story of its fascinating past.

Dejima

For some 220 years from 1639, Japan's only window to the West was the Dutch trading post on the island of Dejima in the bay.
En route to Graba-en by tram.

Graba-en (Glover Garden)

In the Meiji period, European merchants lived in Nagasaki in colonial splendour. One such was the Scotsman Thomas Glover (1838–1911), who supplied arms to the rebels opposing the shogun, helped build Japan's first railway and married a geisha. His house and those of other merchants are in this park.

Graba-en, 10 minutes by tram south of station. Open: Mar–Nov daily 8am–6pm; 8.30am–5pm in winter. Admission charge.

Heiwa Koen (Peace Park)

The second atomic bomb fell on a heavily populated working-class area, killing 150,000 people. The peace museum, renovated for the 50th anniversary of the ending of the war, contains a simple and shocking collection of relics, with material on Japan's war role.

Nagasaki kokusai bunka kaikan (International Culture Hall), 10 minutes by tram north of station. Tel: 0958 44 1231. Open: daily 9am–6pm. Admission charge.

Koushi-byo (Confucian Shrine and Museum of Chinese History)

The Confucian shrine is a glorious building with a brilliant yellow roof made of Beijing tiles. The museum contains artefacts from the Beijing National Museum.

Next to Graba-en. Tel: 0958 24 4022. Open: daily 8.30am–5pm. Admission charge.

Sofukuji

Nagasaki's temple area is well worth exploring. Sofukuji is the highlight, founded by Chinese residents in 1629, with a wonderful Ming-dynasty gateway.

Behind Koushi-byo. Open: daily 8am–5pm. Admission charge.

Nagasaki is in western Kyushu. Accessible by plane; 2 hours south of Fukuoka by train. Tourist information office in station. Tel: 0958 26 9407.

The Ryukyu Islands

The Ryukyus are more like a South Sea paradise than a part of Japan. This chain of islands, with lush palm groves, white beaches and brilliant blue seas, stretches for nearly 1,000km (620 miles) between the southern tip of Kyushu and Taiwan in the East China Sea. Most of the archipelago comes under the Japanese prefecture of Okinawa.

For centuries Okinawa was an independent kingdom, with its capital at **Shuri** (on the island of Okinawa) and a fascinating culture. It has had a long and troubled relationship with Japan. Despite terrible destruction during World War II, some of its distinctive and colourful architecture, music, art and crafts remain. Okinawa's sultry climate and languid lifestyle make it the most exotic place you will visit in Japan. But go soon – the region is fast being turned into a theme park for Japanese holidaymakers.

Aka-jima

A tiny island close to **Naha**, Aka-jima is home to a sleepy village which consists mainly of divers. The beaches are pure white sand, and there are some lovely forest walks and scenic kayaking trips to be made to other, pretty, uninhabited islands.

1½ hours by ferry west of Naha.

Iriomote-jima

Iriomote is Japan's last frontier. Blanketed in dense tropical rainforest, it offers wonderful hiking, a river trip up a mini-Amazon, and some of the best scuba diving in Asia. Divers come specially to see the giant manta rays. If you are lucky, you may also spot the extremely rare Okinawan wildcat.

1 hour by ferry west of Ishigaki.

Ishigaki-jima

Ishigaki is the gateway to the most distant and remote of the Ryukyu Islands – the Yaeyamas, which include Taketomi and Iriomote. It has tropical scenery, glorious beaches and fine diving.

Accessible by plane; 20 hours by ferry southwest of Naha.

Kume-jima

Much of Kume-jima is breathtakingly beautiful, with rows of sugar cane, Ryukyu pines and red-tiled roofs. The **Uezu House**, the oldest remaining traditional Okinawan house, belonged to the local lords and dates from 1726. Kume-jima is famous for its beautiful silk pongee fabrics.

Accessible by plane; 3½ hours by ferry west of Naha.
Uezu House, Gushikawa Village, 5 minutes by bus from Nakadomari Town. Open: daily 9am–5pm. Admission charge.

Miyako-jima

This idyllic island is the core of the Miyako group, eight islands between Okinawa and the Yaeyamas, with their own distinct culture. If you come during the low spring tides, you can see the huge Yaebishi reef emerging from the sea like a phantom island.

Accessible by plane; 10 hours by ferry southwest of Naha.

Okinawa-jima

Any visit to the islands begins at **Naha**, the capital of Okinawa island, the largest and most important in the chain. A lively city with a tropical atmosphere,

Naha is less frenetic and more relaxed than mainland Japan.

Don't miss nearby **Shuri**, the capital of ancient Okinawa. The castle and great ceremonial gate (Shurei-no Mon) are inevitably post-war reconstructions, but, close to the originals, they communicate the exotic flavour of this once great kingdom. Outside Naha is fine countryside; the north of the island is particularly unspoilt. Look for the castle ruins at **Nakagusuku** (1448), on a hilltop in central Okinawa, and **Nakijin** (14th century), on the Motobu peninsula.

Shuri, 25 minutes by bus from central Naha. Nakagusuku, 45 minutes by bus from Naha. Tel: 098 935 3347.
Nakijin, 3½ hours by bus from Naha. The latter two are open: daily 9am–6pm (till 5.30pm in winter). Admission charge.

Glorious seascapes surround the Ryukyu Islands

Shuri Castle

Saga

The Saga area is home to three celebrated pottery towns. **Karatsu** produces elegant muted stoneware, while **Imari** and **Arita** make the country's most famous porcelain.
Northern Kyushu. 2–3 hours southwest of Fukuoka by train and bus.

Takachiho

Takachiho is a small town set in lush countryside, where terraced paddy fields climb the foothills of craggy peaks. According to myth, the sun goddess once hid in a cave in one of its picturesque gorges. Nothing could persuade her to come out, until a young goddess performed an erotic dance which set the gods laughing so uproariously that the sun goddess peeped out – and the world was saved. The cave is still there, with an atmospheric old shrine above it. You can watch the nightly performance of sacred dance (Iwato Kagura) at **Takachiho Jinja** (Takachiho Shrine), culminating in an erotic dance as entertaining as the one which lured the sun goddess out.
Central Kyushu, 2 hours by bus southeast of Mount Aso. Iwato Kagura at Takachiho Jinja, nightly, 8–9pm. Admission charge.

Usuki

An interesting side trip from Beppu, Usuki is a small town with some of the finest and most ancient stone Buddhas in Japan.
Eastern Kyushu, 40 minutes by train southeast of Beppu.
Usuki sekibutsu (stone Buddhas), 20 minutes by bus from station.
Open: daily dawn–dusk.
Admission charge.

Yanagawa

Yanagawa means 'Willow River'. Its roads are intertwined with moats and canals lined with willows. Boatmen in straw hats and happi coats punt you around the reed-filled waterways.

Northern Kyushu, 1 hour south of Fukuoka by train.

Yufuin

While its neighbour, the more famous Beppu (*see pp136–7*), is brash and neon-lit, Yufuin is a rustic retreat surrounded by mountains and swaying bamboo groves – in fact everything you ever imagined a Japanese spa to be.

Eastern Kyushu, 1 hour by bus west of Beppu.

Monumental stone Buddha in Usuki

The tropical south

Getting away from it all

Escape from Japan's bustling cities and heavy traffic and you will be surprised by the array of breathtaking views, peaceful parks and wildlife off the beaten track. The country's climate ranges from temperate in Hokkaido to subtropical in Okinawa, giving the island nation some extraordinarily different landscapes; from snowcapped mountains and lakes in the north to beaches and palm trees in the south.

NORTHERN ESCAPES

One of Japan's best-kept secrets is its expanses of wild, unspoilt country. Head away from the industrial heartland to the sparsely populated mountains of the north, where there are endless tracts of glorious alpine and volcanic scenery, with unlimited opportunities for walking, mountain-climbing or skiing. Northern roads tend to be fairly empty, except in summer, so driving is a viable way of seeing the countryside.

For Japanese, a journey to the mountains invariably incorporates a visit to a hot spring. Japan being a volatile volcanic country, there is sulphurous hot water gushing out of the ground wherever you go. You will doubtless quickly pick up the Japanese habit of enjoying a long hot soak after a strenuous day's travelling or hiking.

Hokkaido
Akan National Park

Akan has three magical crater lakes. Lake Kusshuro is vast and serene.

Lake Mashu, deep, mysterious and rimmed by steep, forested slopes, was called the 'Lake of the Devil' by the Ainu. It is often obscured by clouds, but when visible is miraculously beautiful. Lake Akan was a centre for Ainu culture and is home to a mysterious green algae, the *marimo* weed. There is little hiking in the area; all three lakes are accessible by bus or car (*see also p67*).

Daisetsuzan National Park

Daisetsuzan is Japan's largest national park and a paradise for hikers. Most people begin their visit at **Sounkyo Gorge**, a dramatic ravine with plunging waterfalls and fantastically shaped rocks. A road runs the length of the gorge, or you can hire a bicycle or walk. You can also begin the climb at the mountain spa of Asahidake. From here a cable car takes you up into another world where alpine plants bloom against forbidding volcanic slopes. Hiking trails criss-cross the area. The seven-hour walk between Sounkyo and

Asahidake follows a high, windswept ridge, skirting the rims of several craters (*see also p67*).

Rishiri-Rebun National Park

Hikers visit these northernmost islands of Hokkaido to trek to the summit of Rishiri, a spectacular volcanic cone rising straight out of the sea. You can also walk the length of Rebun, along clifftops and shingly beaches. In summer the islands are brilliant with wild flowers (*see also p79*).

Shikotsu-Toya National Park

The most accessible of Hokkaido's national parks, Shikotsu-Toya centres around two beautiful crater lakes, Lake Toya and Lake Shikotsu. It has something for everyone – spectacular mountain scenery, hiking trails, volcanoes to climb and the region's most famous spa, Noboribetsu (*see also p76*). But what most visitors come to see are two very active volcanoes: Showa Shinzan, which thrust its way out of a farmer's field in 1943, and Mount Usu, which last erupted in 1977.

Shiretoko National Park

Roads extend only part-way along the Shiretoko Peninsula, in the far north of Hokkaido, and hikers who venture into the interior are warned to beware of bears. This is one area in Japan where bears still roam free; for the last ten years they have been protected. The small town of Utoro, where explorations of the peninsula begin, is ugly but fun,

full of Japanese who have fled from the rat race of Tokyo (*see also p78*).

Tohoku

Most of Tohoku district is a gigantic national park, mile upon mile of rolling hills covered in impenetrable forest, interspersed with lakes, rivers and lush countryside carpeted with paddy fields. The **Towada-Hachimantai National Park**, in the northern part of the region, is centred around two pleasant caldera lakes, Lake Towada and Lake Tazawa (*see also pp78–9*).

SACRED MOUNTAINS

Since ancient times the Japanese have believed that the gods live in beautiful natural surroundings – in particular on mountaintops. Traditionally, going on holiday meant a pilgrimage. This entailed making the climb, often long and dangerous, to the top of a sacred mountain to commune with the gods.

Lake Mashu, Akan National Park, in winter

Today if you walk in the mountains in summer, you will find yourself in company with many white-clad pilgrims, wearing bells and carrying staffs. Along the way the paths are strewn with cairns, stone images and small shrines, while the summit of practically every mountain is crowned with a *torii* and shrine. The pilgrimage season and the popular time for climbing sacred mountains is July and August. In the winter the mountains are snowbound.

To the Japanese, the mountains are traditionally female and, therefore, jealous of other females. Until recently most sacred mountains were closed to women: Mount Omine, the holiest of all, still is.

The most famous sacred mountain is Mount Fuji (*see pp56–7 & pp58–9*). Other celebrated mountains include Takachiho (*see p144*), where the wind god Ninigi first alighted to rule earth; Mount Koya, the headquarters of the esoteric Shingon Buddhist sect – 123 temples scattered across a wild mountaintop not far from Osaka (*see pp107–8*); and Mount Hiei, in Kyoto (*see* Enryakuji, *p82*).

Dewa Sanzan (Three Mountains of Dewa)

Dewa Sanzan is one of Japan's most spectacular and famous sacred mountains and the headquarters of the mountaineering ascetics called *yamabushi*. The pilgrimage begins with the lowest of the three mountains that compose Dewa Sanzan, Mount Haguro. You climb through ancient cryptomeria forests, up endless stone steps. The second mountain, Gassan ('Moon Mountain'), is a long hard trek across marshes and grass-covered slopes, with splendid views across the surrounding country. Finally pilgrims make the steep descent to **Mount Yudono**, to worship at the sacred hot spring there. Today, for pilgrims with less time, there is a bus to the summit of Haguro and another to Yudono (*see also p67*).

Omine-san (Mount Omine)

There are two routes to Japan's most sacred mountain, Mount Omine. One begins at Kimpu-jinja (Kimpu Shrine, *see p119*) on the top of Mount Yoshino, where a stone post proclaims in Japanese 'off limits to females'. The other begins at Kumano, the centre for the mountaineering priests of medieval times. From either direction it is a day-long hike to the top of Mount Omine. Pilgrims are expected to observe disciplines such as being hung by their heels over a cliff, to remind them of the frailty of their existence. For women, there are plenty of mountain walks skirting the forbidden Omine.

Osore-zan (Mount Osore)

Osore-zan means 'Terrible Mountain', and it is not difficult to believe, as many Japanese still do, that the souls of the dead gather there. It is a weird and desolate volcanic landscape of rocks, ash and rubble, where nothing grows and sulphur-laden steam stains the rocks yellow. The best time to visit is in July, during the four-day mediums' festival, the stars of which are blind women mediums. Japanese arrive in their thousands to commune with the souls of their dead. You can stay in the temple lodgings with the pilgrims and enjoy the very primitive mixed baths (*see also p76*).

IN THE SOUTH

Japan's south is semi-tropical. Here life goes on at a different pace, amid the sultry heat and palm trees, often in the shadow of active volcanoes. The change begins just south of the industrial belt along the top of Kyushu.

Kyushu

Kyushu's three national parks have beautiful and contrasting scenery. The centre of the island is dominated by the truly spectacular Aso-Kuju National Park (*see pp134, 136*), spread around the vast crater of Aso with its smouldering inner volcanoes. You can drive along the Yamanami Highway, which links Aso with Yufuin, through panoramic mountain scenery and past Mount Kuju, Kyushu's highest peak at 1,788m (5,866ft). Back roads will take you past timeless mountain villages, terraced paddy fields and thatched farmhouses. To the east, you can hike or drive through the remote, corrugated hills of the Kunisaki Peninsula (*see p141*), and explore its tiny villages, ancient temples and stone

Tropical ferns on the Ryukyu Islands

Getting away from it all

Buddhas. Some of the most glorious landscape in Japan is in the Kirishima range in southern Kyushu (*see p139*). You can hike across the chain of volcanic peaks or laze in the outdoor hot springs on the lower slopes.

The Ryukyu Islands

For those in search of a tropical paradise, the Ryukyus are the place to go. Despite increased tourism, there are still plenty of unspoilt beaches, blue seas, coral reefs and tiny villages of red-tiled houses. Leave the capital Naha and the main island of Okinawa behind you and head for the outer islands: Kume-jima with its wonderful beaches; tiny Aka-jima, with its picturesque trails and peaceful atmosphere; and Iriomote-jima, Japan's last true wilderness (*see also p142*).

Shopping

Japan is the ultimate consumer society. In boom times and recessions, Japan's shoppers carry on spending. Twin loves of innovation and fashion keep the people purchasing. The quality of service makes shopping a joy, from the uniformed girl who bows you on to the escalator in a department store to the friendly staff in small local stores.

Set aside time for window shopping. Unfortunately, not much is really cheap in Japan, but you will find surprising bargains. For instance, don't assume that designer fashion is out of reach: Issey Miyake clothes are cheaper in Japan than in the West, and brands like Burberry sell affordable labels such as Burberry Black in Japan only.

There is no Sunday closing in Japan; in fact, Japanese shops are busiest on Sundays. Department stores are generally open from 10am to 7pm and close one day a week, usually Wednesday or Thursday. Other stores may stay open much longer – Tokyo is gradually becoming an open-round-the-clock city.

Tax-free shopping

Tax-free shopping is available in department and other large stores, including discount shops where you can buy a wide range of electronic goods and cameras. Present your receipt and passport at a special desk for an immediate refund. In addition, most large stores that cater for tourists usually have one or more floors of export goods. If you present your passport when paying you will be given a discount.

Department stores

The first place to look for any item is a department store. There are branches of most in every major city. **Mitsukoshi** and **Takashimaya** are the oldest and most prestigious; look there for traditional silks, kimonos and handicrafts. **Seibu** is the most youthful and adventurous, the place for avant-garde design. **Isetan** is another store that is good for fashion. The basements of most department stores are foodie heavens. Known as *depachika*, they are a riot of colours and aromas. They are good for finding edible souvenirs or for a cheap but tasty lunch.

WHAT TO BUY
Electronic goods and cameras

The range of electronic goods and cameras in Japan is huge. You can pick up the latest state-of-the-art model before it arrives in the West. But don't expect to save any money: prices may turn out to be no lower than at home.

To ensure compatibility, buy only the export model of sophisticated equipment; you can also buy adaptors suitable for each country. Akihabara has several stores (such as LAOX) that stock export models of electronic goods and have English-speaking staff.

Handicrafts

Japanese handicrafts are of the highest quality and they make wonderful souvenirs and gifts.

Kimonos come in a wide variety of prices and qualities. New kimonos are exorbitantly expensive (¥100,000+) but second-hand ones are quite reasonable. You can buy kimono silk (the Nishijin area in Kyoto is famous for this) and obi, the thick brocade that wraps the waist. *Yukata*, blue-and-white cotton summer kimonos, are especially popular. Besides scouring stores specifically serving tourists, look for such items in general stores, department stores, even flea markets.

Japanese pottery is made locally in pottery villages including Bizen, Iga, Karatsu and Hagi; Kyoto is the home of Kiyomizu ware, while Kutani porcelain is produced in the Kanazawa area.

You will also find wonderful dolls; traditional accessories like bamboo combs and hairpins; the most beautiful handmade paper in the world, used to make oiled paper umbrellas, lanterns,

fans and kites; traditional lacquerware; and pearls. *Netsuke*, tiny exquisitely carved toggles, have become collectors' items. Woodblock prints (*ukiyo-e*) vary enormously in price; there are bargains to be had in the second-hand bookshop areas of Tokyo and Kyoto.

WHERE TO SHOP
Tokyo
Antiques and souvenirs
Asakusabashi area Traditional doll and toy shops.
Hanae Mori Building Over 30 antique shops in the basement.
Hanae Mori Building B1, Omotesando. Tel: 03 3406 1021. Open: daily.
Kiddyland Five floors of some of the most unusual and interesting souvenirs you can find.
Close to Oriental Bazaar, Harajuku. Tel: 03 3409 3431.
Kurofune High-quality antiques sourced from around Japan.
7-7-4 Roppongi. Tel: 03 3479 1552. Open: Mon–Sat.

Buy anime figurines in Akihabara

Nakamise-dori A wide range of traditional goods.
Oriental Bazaar Souvenirs of every conceivable kind.
5-9-13 Jingumae, Harajuku.
Tel: 03 3400 3933. Open: Fri–Wed.

Books and records
The most famous bookshop area is Jimbocho. Most shops stock only Japanese books.
Kinokuniya *3-17-7 Shinjuku.*
Tel: 03 3354 0131.
Kitazawa Shoten *Yasukuni-dori.*
Tel: 03 3263 0011.
Maruzen *Oazo Building, 1-6-4 Marunouchi. Tel: 03 5218 5100.*
Open: Mon–Sat 10am–7pm.
Tower Records *Just north of JR Shibuyu station. Tel: 03 3496 3661.*
Open: daily 10am–11pm.

Cameras and electronic goods
Akihabara area Look for signs to **Akihabara Electric City** in Akihabara train station. Bring your passport for tax-free shopping.
Bic Camera To the south of Yurakucho station. Claims to be the cheapest camera store in Japan. *Tel: 03 5221 1111.*
Yodobashi Camera Tokyo's most famous camera shop; huge discounts.
1-11-1 Nishi-Shinjuku. Tel: 03 3346 1010. www.yodobashi.com

Fashion and design
Ginza Several large department stores and luxury shops, though prices are generally higher than in other parts of Tokyo. **Shibuya** offers a wide range of fashion shops, **Harajuku** caters for young fashion, and **Aoyama** has the best designer boutiques.
Laforet Building Houses a range of boutiques. Walk towards Omotesando from Harajuku station and turn left at the crossroads with a GAP on it.
Tel: 03 3472 0411.
Marronnier Gate A gleaming new shopping complex in Ginza.
2-2-14 Ginza. www.marronniergate.com
Parco, **Seibu** and the **109 Building** are close to the subway station in Shibuya.

Flea markets
Nogi Shrine, Roppongi 2nd Sunday of each month.
Togo Shrine, Harajuku 1st and 4th Sunday of each month.

Kyoto
In Kyoto's backstreets are elegant old shops selling traditional arts and crafts.
Shinmonzen Street, north of Gion, has Japan's greatest concentration of antique shops.

Nishiki Market, just north of Shijo-agaru, is unmissable for foodies. Flea markets include **Kitano-Tenmangu Shrine** (*see p86*), 25th of every month; **Toji** (*see p93*), 21st of every month.

Osaka
Shinsaibashi is the classiest shopping area. **Nipponbashi Den Den Town** (Nipponbashi and Nankai Namba stations) has 300 shops selling duty-free electronic goods.

Entertainment

The Japanese play as hard as they work. There is an enormous variety of entertainment on offer in every city, from traditional Japanese theatre, music and dance to the latest avant-garde performance art or techno-rock. Many Western performers begin their tours in Japan, where they are guaranteed huge audiences. Concerts, theatre and cinema are expensive, but the quality and facilities are among the best in the world.

In Tokyo, you can dance the night away at one of the city's many clubs or karaoke bars. Most Japanese bars/clubs stay open until 5 or 6 in the morning, but most trains stop running from around midnight.

Information

Every major city has several English-language newspapers and magazines providing listings in detail. In Tokyo, the most comprehensive is the weekly *Metropolis*. There are also listings in the daily *Japan Times*, and several free English-language publications (which come in and go out of circulation rapidly), available from the Tourist Information Centre (TIC), and in hotels and pubs.

In central Japan, *Kansai Scene* and the *Mainichi Daily News* keep you up to date with Kyoto, Osaka and Kobe. The *Kyoto Monthly Guide* and *Kyoto Visitor's Guide*, both available at Kyoto TIC, are also useful. *Nagoya Eyes* is the best guide to Nagoya. In Kanazawa,

look out for *Cosmos* every month. In Hiroshima, the fortnightly *Link-up* has listings for the area. Fukuoka's lively nightlife is covered by the monthly *Rainbow*, free from Rainbow Plaza in the IMS Building. Look out too for *Radar*, Fukuoka's trendy listings paper, published on the 25th of each month. All listings magazines are available from major bookshops selling English books.

Cinema

Many cinema buffs know Japan primarily through the wonderful films of directors such as Akira Kurosawa, Yasujiro Ozu and Juzo Itami. New films by top directors are sometimes given special showings with English subtitles; see listings magazines for details.

RESERVATIONS

Make reservations through your hotel, at **PIA**, **Saisons** or **Playguide** ticket agencies in main stations and the ground floor or basement of department stores.

Clubs, live houses, bars

There are surely more nightspots per square kilometre in Japan than anywhere else in the world, from the ultra-glamorous to the downright funky.

TOKYO

A971 Popular bar, especially with flirting singles.
Tokyo Midtown. Tel: 03 5413 3210.
Ageha Huge multi-floor club complete with pool. Frequently showcases international DJs.
Tel: 03 5534 1515. www.ageha.com
Blue Note Tokyo Big jazz acts at big prices.
10-minute walk southeast of Omotesando subway. Tel: 03 5485 0088.
Kamiya Bar Nostalgic dining bar with over a century of history, best known for its Denki Bran drink.
At Asakusa subway. Tel: 03 3841 5400.
Loft A great live house.
Kabukicho, Shinjuku. Tel: 03 3365 0698.
New York Bar 42nd floor of the Tokyo Park Hyatt hotel.
Shinjuku. Tel: 03 5323 3458.
Paddy Foley's Popular expat pub on Roppongi-dori.
5 minutes south of Roppongi subway. Tel: 03 3423 0988.
Popeye Seventy Japanese beers on tap.
South of Ryogoku station. Tel: 03 3633 2120.
Pub Cardinal Marunouchi Laid-back lounge bar with outdoor terrace.
Tokyo Building, 2-7-3 Marunouchi. Tel: 03 5222 1521.
www.miyoshi-grp.com/cardinal/pcm

Star Bar Japan's top cocktail bar.
Ginza Itchome station. Tel: 03 3535 8005.
What the Dickens Spacious but busy pub that hosts small live acts.
3-minute walk northwest of Ebisu subway. Tel: 03 3780 2099.

OSAKA

Blue Note Osaka Jazz club.
Ax Building B1, 2-3-21 Sonezaki-Shinchi, Kita-ku. Tel: 06 6342 7722.
Ozone Funky club with regular DJs.
2-9-36 Nishi-Shinsaibashi, Chuo-ku. Tel: 06 6213 2994.
Peko Quiet, spacious and has an extensive selection of Japanese craft beers, whisky and cocktails.
Chayamachi 13-9. Tel: 06 6371 3321.

Geisha dancing and traditional arts

Geisha are hired through teahouses, which only deal with well-connected regulars. Some ryokan or high-end hotels will be able to arrange for geisha to join you for a dinner. It's much easier to attend one of the dance performances in Atami (*see p50*) or Kyoto (*see below*).

KYOTO

Gion Corner Traditional arts: tea ceremony, flower arrangement, music, theatre, dance.
Yasaka Hall, Gion. Tel: 075 561 1119.
Performances: 1 Mar–29 Nov.
Miyako odori (Cherry blossom dancing), Gion Kobu-Kaburenjo Theatre Performances by *maiko*

(trainee geisha) four times a day throughout April.
Gion Corner. Tel: 075 561 1115.

Hostess bars

These are largely for well-heeled and well-oiled businessmen; best to try on someone else's expense account.

Karaoke bars

Most karaoke is performed in private with friends in a 'karaoke box', though some bars offer stages for public humiliation. Look for major karaoke chains such as Big Echo, and be wary of anywhere labelled 'snack' – these are quasi-hostess bars with outrageous fees for drinks.

TOKYO

Big Echo Outlets all over Japan and a good selection of Western songs.
Tel: 03 5770 7700.
Fiesta International Karaoke Bar Many English songs – plus funny costumes.
7-9-3 Roppongi. Tel: 03 5410 3008.
www.fiesta-roppongi.com

Music

Watch out for concerts by Japan's world-famous composers, and top-notch orchestras; concerts at the NHK Hall in Shibuya, Tokyo.

Performance art, contemporary theatre and *buto* (dance)

There is a strong avant-garde movement in Japan, and much performance art, contemporary theatre and dance, being generally wordless, is easy to follow.
Buto is Japan's own distinctive form of contemporary dance.

Theatre

Traditional Japanese theatre is very stylised. Kabuki portrays events from Japanese history, with females played by male actors. Noh comes from Kyoto and is performed by actors in masks. *Bunraku* is puppet theatre from Osaka.

TOKYO

National Theatre Noh and kabuki.
Subway: Akasaka-mitsuke.
Tel: 03 3265 7411.

KYOTO

Kanze Kaikan Noh Theatre Noh performances fourth Sunday of each month except July.
South of Heian Shrine, near Higashiyama Sanjo tram stop. Tel: 075 771 6114.
Kongo Noh Stage Noh performances fourth Sunday of each month except August.
5-minute walk from Shijo subway.
Tel: 075 712 7190.
Minamiza Since the closure of Tokyo's Kabuki Theatre, the nation's top venue.
Next to Keihan-shijo station.
Tel: 075 561 1115.

OSAKA

National Bunraku Theatre
Performances in January, April, June, July, September, November.
At Nipponbashi subway, Central Osaka.
Tel: 06 6212 2531.

Youth culture

Japan may be a nation steeped in tradition, but it is also a country that is becoming famous for its fashions, which break with convention and can, in fact, border on the bizarre. Tokyo is the place to see clothing at its most innovative and progressive. Tourists and Japanese alike flock to Harajuku and Shibuya, and in particular to Yoyogi Park, to see the most weird and wonderful of clothing creations.

Every Sunday afternoon at Jingu Bridge, the entrance to Yoyogi Park just in front of the gateway towards Meiji Shrine (*see p43*), 'Goth lolis' and cosplay fans (*see also p15*) gather to meet friends and to express their sense of style to the world. Goth loli is short for 'Gothic Lolita', and these grim babes sport almost all black, from their frilly dresses and umbrellas to their crosses and the miniature

Checking in with friends while hanging out on Jingu Bridge on a Sunday

Dramatic make-up adds to the look

coffins they carry around. The unique costumes don't stop there, though: you will see any number of young Japanese men and women dressed as the opposite sex, plenty sporting bright red hair and even some giving out free hugs. Many of these youths come from the furthest corners of Tokyo to meet friends and hang out on Jingu Bridge.

Further into Yoyogi Park on a Sunday afternoon, you will always find the rockabillies clad in leather, grooving to old-time rock and roll.

Shibuya's 109 Building and Harajuku's Takeshita Street are the capital's two youth fashion meccas. The 109 Building in particular is known for starting trends, and the shop assistants here can become minor celebrities, offering tips in magazines and going on to launch their own lines.

Akihabara has also become a youth capital of sorts, drawing the *otaku* (obsessive geeks) with multi-storey manga emporiums and huge electronics stores. It's also home to the most maid cafés and their spin-offs, including butler cafés, cross-dressing butler cafés, and *tsundere* cafés, where staff deliver a frosty reception and ice-cold service, then switch to exaggerated fawning as you try to leave.

In recent years, as Akihabara has become more of a tourist attraction, the true geeks have started to go elsewhere, including Ikebukuro and Nakano, in the west of the city, but Akihabara is still the best place to immerse yourself in the quirkier side of Japanese youth culture.

Children

When it comes to children, forget about temples and shrines and look to modern hi-tech Japan. There are state-of-the-art game parks, theme parks, amusement parks, aquariums and planetariums, all done with Japanese finesse and attention to detail and using all the resources of Japanese technology. These are some of the best in the world. Japan provides a wonderful opportunity for your children (and you) to try out the latest games years before they arrive in the West.

Tokyo and surroundings

Make your first stop the Ueno area (*see p30*), with its zoo (*www.tokyo-zoo.net*), amusement park and many museums – perfect for a rainy day.

Joypolis (Sega Game Park)

An indoor game park from Sega, creators of Sonic the Hedgehog, that's a whole lot more active than your average games arcade. Strap yourself into the snowboard simulator 'Halfpipe Canyon', ride the mini indoor rollercoaster 'Spin Bullet', but keep the kids away from the genuinely scary walk-through haunted house 'Inbikisou Taidouhen'.
*Odaiba Kaihin-Koen station.
Tel: 03 5500 1801. Open: daily 10am–11pm. Admission charge.*

Kidzania

A miniature world complete with buildings, roads, shops and traffic. Children can play at being policemen, doctors, firemen and more.
1st Floor Urban Dock Lala Port Toyosu. Tel: 03 3536 2100. www.kidzania.co.jp. Open: daily 10am–3pm & 4–9pm.

Kodomo no Shiro (Children's Castle)

A wonderland for children, with music rooms, video rooms and play areas.
*5-53-1 Jingumae, Shibuya-ku, 5-minute walk from Omotesando subway.
Tel: 03 3797 5666. www.kodomono-shiro.or.jp. Open: daily 9am–6pm.*

Kokuritsu Kagaku Hakubutsukan (National Science Museum)

Traditional science museum (*see p40*).

Tokyo Disney Resort®

Combines two theme parks (Tokyo Disneyland® and DisneySEA®) plus hotels, shops, restaurants and a multiplex cinema.
1-1 Maihama, Urayasu-shi, Chiba-ken, train or bus from Tokyo station. General information in English (tel: 045 683 3777). Opening days & hours vary with year and season.

Tokyo-to Jido-kan (Tokyo Metropolitan Children's Hall)

Seven floors full of every imaginable display and scientific toy.

7-minute walk from Shibuya station east exit. Tel: 03 3409 6361. Open: daily 9am–5pm. Free admission.

Osaka
Kaiyukan Aquarium
This vast aquarium in Osaka Port opened in 1990 and features a glass-walled underwater tunnel that takes visitors 'inside' the aquarium.
1-1-10 Kaigan-dori, Chuo-ku, Osaka-ko subway. Tel: 06 6576 5501. www.kaiyukan.com. Open: daily 10am–8pm. Admission charge.
Panasonic Square
A chance to play with the latest hi-tech from the Matsushita Electric Group.
National Tower Building, 2F, Twin Towers, Osaka Business Park. Tel: 06 6949 2111. www.panasonic.co.jp/center/osaka. Open: daily 10am–6pm.

Spaworld
Spas, baths and an amusement pool with waterslides.
3-4-24 Ebisu-higashi, Naniwa-ku. Tel: 06 6631 0001. www.spaworld.co.jp. Open: daily 10am–midnight. Admission charge.

Fukuoka
Space World
Your chance to experience anti-gravity, go through (abbreviated) astronauts' training, stay in Star Lodge and visit the Space Museum and the Galaxy Theatre.
900-1 Edamitsu, Yawata Higashi-ku, Kita-Kyushu. Tel: 093 672 3600. www.spaceworld.co.jp. Open: mid-Jul–end Aug daily 9am–9pm; Sept–Jun daily 9, 9.30 or 10am–4.30, 5 or 6pm. Closed: 11–28 Jan; 1–16 Jul; 1–22 Dec. Admission charge.

Ginkgo trees in front of the National Science Museum

Children

Sport and leisure

Until the arrival of Westerners, there were no team sports in Japan. Instead, Japanese athletes developed their skills in one-to-one combat, like sumo wrestling, and the martial arts of judo and kendo.

SUMO

No one can fail to spot a sumo wrestler. These gentle giants are usually over 180cm (6ft) tall, weigh anything up to 240kg (38 stone) and are national heroes. Sumo itself is not a mere sport but Japan's *kokugi* or 'national skill'. It has its origins in religious ritual and some Shinto shrines still hold sacred contests. The sumo ring is marked, like a Shinto shrine, by a thick rope and is purified with salt before a match.

The object of the match is either to push the opponent out of the ring or to topple him so that any part of his body other than the soles of his feet touches the ground. But the final clash is only a small part of the spectacle; the ritual that precedes it is equally important.

Sumo wrestlers have a special diet and exercise regime to produce their enormous size. They are superb athletes, astonishingly limber, and much of that weight is solid muscle.

Sumo tournaments last 15 days and start on the second Sunday of every other month. They are held in:

Tokyo January, May and September at Kokugikan Stadium, *Ryogoku station. Tel: 03 3866 8700* for tickets.

Nagoya July at Aichi Prefectural Gymnasium, *1-1 Ninomaru, Naka-ku. Tel: 052 971 0015.*

Osaka March at Prefectural Gymnasium, *2 Shin Kawamachi, Naniwa-ku. Tel: 06 6631 0120.*

Fukuoka November at International Centre, *2-2 Chikko Honmachi, Hakata-ku. Tel: 092 272 1111.*

You can reserve tickets through your hotel, at Playguide ticket agencies or by visiting *www.sumo.goo.ne.jp*

BUDO (TRADITIONAL MARTIAL ARTS)

Traditionally martial arts originated as a training for samurai warriors, designed to transform the body, forge the mind and build up fighting spirit. They sharpen concentration so that movement and response become intuitive.

Aikido

The modern sport of aikido – 'the way of harmonious spirit' – was founded in the 1920s by Morihei Ueshiba (1883–1970). It is a method of non-violent self-defence which involves making use of the opponent's energy in order to make him fall over. For details, contact:

International Aikido Federation
17–18 Wakamatsu-cho, Shinjuku-ku, Tokyo. Tel: 03 3203 9236.
www.aikido-international.org

Judo

Judo – 'the way of softness' – is the best-known martial art and a recognised Olympic sport. You can study judo or watch from the spectators' gallery at the

All-Japan Judo Federation
Kodokan, 1-16-30 Kasuga, Bunkyo-ku, Tokyo.
Tel: 03 3818 4199.
www.judo.or.jp

Karate

Karate – 'empty hand' – is a method of fighting with the hands and feet. It originated in India and reached Japan via China and Okinawa.

World Union of Karate-do Organisations
Sempaku Shinkokai Building, 1-15-16 Toranomon, Minato-ku, Tokyo.
Tel: 03 5534 1951.

Kendo

Kendo – 'the way of the sword' – is a form of fencing practised with bamboo staves or wooden swords.

All Japan Kendo Federation
Nippon Budokan, Kitanomaru Park, Tokyo. Tel: 03 3211 5804.

Kyudo

Kyudo is 'the way of archery', as immortalised in E Herrigel's book *Zen in the Art of Archery* (1953). The aim is spiritual – to develop such Zen-like singleness of concentration that the arrow finds its own way to the bullseye.

All Japan Kyudo Federation
Kishi Memorial Hall, Jinnan, 1-1-1 Shibuya-ku, Tokyo. Tel: 03 3481 2387.
www.kyudo.jp

MODERN SPORTS

Baseball is far and away the most popular sport in Japan, though there are also professional or semi-

A kendo duel

Sport and leisure

professional leagues for football, American football and basketball.

Baseball

Baseball hit Japan in 1873. Ever since then young lads have been out on the street, wielding bats and pitching balls. The baseball season is April to October and there are two professional leagues, the Central and the Pacific. At the end of the season, the winners of each league have a seven-match play-off for the Japan Series. Tokyo teams dominate both leagues. The main venues are:

Tokyo Dome

Home of Japan's best-loved team, the Yomiuri Giants.

1-3-61 Korakuen, Tokyo.
Tel: 03 5800 9999.

Nissei Stadium

Where the high-school baseball tournament, a much celebrated event, is held in August.

Osaka. Tel: 06 6941 5505.

Fukuoka Dome

Home of the Daiei Hawks, a team worth keeping an eye on.

2-2-2 Jigyohama, Fukuoka.
Tel: 092 847 1006.

Football

The J League kicked off in 1990 and football frenzy has gripped Japan ever since, especially after Japan co-hosted the 2002 World Cup. Football stadiums have sprung up all over the country, and, instead of wielding baseball bats, many Japanese children (and adults) are now kicking footballs. There are

16 teams in the league, of which the strongest are currently the **Kashima Antlers**, **Urawa Reds**, **Gamba Osaka** and **Kawasaki Frontale**. Information in English is available from:

J League

Sakurai Building 4F, 3-19-8 Uchikanda, Chiyoda-ku, Tokyo. Tel: 03 3257 4871.
www.j-league.or.jp

Golf

Golf used to be the preserve of businessmen, but, though it is still expensive, there are now plenty of non-membership golf courses. If you just want to practise your swing, watch out for the many multistorey golf-driving ranges. Contact:

Aqualine Golf Club

Tel: 0438 53 3800.
Email: aqualinegc@accordiagolf.com

Gotemba Golf Club

Challenging greens with spectacular Mount Fuji views.

Tel: 0550 87 1555.
Email: Ben-galloway@gotembagolf.com

Keeping fit

In Tokyo, you can work out at the following:

Golds Gym

Branches throughout Tokyo.

Tel: 03 5766 3131.

Jeff's Fitness

Offers female fitness programmes.

Tel: 090 3903 6390. www.jeffsfitness.com.

Metropolitan Gymnasium

1-17 Sendagaya, Sendagaya station.
Tel: 03 5474 2111.

Abundant snow for winter sports enthusiasts

Tipness

Branches throughout Tokyo.

Tel: 03 5474 3531.

You can also work out at the cheaper XAX chains or at many hotels. Check out reciprocal arrangements with your home health club. Outside Tokyo, choices are more limited. All major hotels issue jogging maps.

Skiing and winter sports

A country of mountains, covered in deep snow from December to March, Japan has some of the world's cheapest skiing – though also surely the most crowded. The main resorts are in Honshu and Hokkaido. For more information, see the Japan National Tourist Office's pamphlet *Skiing in Japan* or visit *www.snowjapan.com*

Watersports

Japan has innumerable fine beaches and ample watersports. The nearest resort to Tokyo is Kamakura, where the sea is full of windsurfers, water-skiers and jet-skiers. The beaches on the Sea of Japan coast are quieter. There are many public pools as well as pools at fitness centres and large hotels.

Food and drink

Japanese food is an adventure in itself. At the top end of the scale it is practically an art form, so beautiful that you can hardly bear to eat it. But there is plenty of good humble hearty fare too. Be prepared for a whole new palate of flavours as well as a new range of extraordinary ingredients – not just raw fish but wild vegetables, tofu (soya-bean curd) in various guises, and even insects.

Types of cuisine

Sashimi

Sashimi is raw fish – the choicest parts of best-quality fish, freshly cut and dipped into soy sauce with a hint of *wasabi* (Japanese horseradish). This is where the chef often shows their artistry, creating a mouthwatering variety of shapes and colours.

Sukiyaki and *shabu-shabu*

Both are made with prime beef, cooked at the table. *Sukiyaki* is sautéed with a rich sweet sauce; *shabu-shabu* is simmered in broth and served with sauces for dipping.

Sushi

Sushi consists of bite-sized chunks of raw fish on vinegar-flavoured rice. Even if you have eaten it at home, you will be amazed at the range of tastes and textures: there is an extraordinary variety of fish and shellfish available in Japan, many of which you will never have tried before. Look out for

conveyor-belt sushi shops (*kaiten-zushi*), where you help yourself to sushi as it glides past and pay by the plate – an economical way to discover which sushi you like.

You can eat sushi with chopsticks or your fingers. Turn it upside down and dip the fish side into soy sauce.

Tempura

Tempura is seafood and vegetables, deep-fried in a light, crisp batter. The best is freshly made before your eyes. Dip in sauce before eating.

Teppanyaki

A *teppanyaki* restaurant is a Japanese steak house. You sit around a large counter topped with a gleaming steel plate, on which the chef grills prime beef, chicken, seafood and vegetables.

Unagi (eel)

Forget jellied eels! Japanese eel is a succulent delicacy, filleted live, grilled over charcoal and brushed with a rich sweet sauce. It is said to have aphrodisiac and energy-giving properties. Not to be missed.

Japanese haute cuisine
Kaiseki

Kaiseki is the ultimate Japanese cuisine. The exclusive restaurants where it is served are called *ryotei*, and the service, dishes and appearance of the food are as important as the flavour. A typical *kaiseki* meal consists of many different bite-sized morsels, each a miniature work of art, perfectly shaped and flavoured.

Shojin ryori (Temple cooking)

As Buddhists, the Japanese evolved a fine tradition of vegetarian cookery, which is served in temples, especially in Kyoto. The cuisine makes much use of soya-bean products – not just tofu but *yuba*, the skin of simmering soya milk and a great delicacy. Watch for *yudofu*,

tofu simmered in broth, and *dengaku*, tofu grilled over charcoal and spread with a sweet, thick bean-curd jam.

Eating cheaply

Despite Japan's reputation for outrageous expense, there is plenty of good, cheap food. There are restaurant arcades on the top floors of every department store and in many stations, which often have enormous underground arcades, full of restaurants.

Most restaurants offer bargain-price set lunches (*teishoku*). Beware of modest-looking backstreet restaurants which do not display prices; they may turn out to be unbelievably expensive.

There is a growing number of vegetarian restaurants in Japan's major cities and various organic, vegetarian retreats around the nation that gave birth to macrobiotics. When in doubt, ask 'Bejitarian no ryori ga arimasu ka?' ('Do you have any vegetarian dishes?').

The Japanese have mastered the art of copying and often do a better job of other countries' cuisines than their home nations. You will find a wide range of Western, Asian and American restaurants in most major cities.

Bento

A bento is a meal in a box. These range from a simple packed lunch to grand meals, beautifully arranged in the compartments of a lacquered container. You can buy *ekiben*, takeaway meals, on stations or in bullet trains.

SAKE

A rice spirit, made from steamed, fermented rice, sake is the drink of the gods. There are often rows of sake casks in front of Shinto shrines. It can be served hot (*atsukan*), cold (*hiyazake*) or at room temperature. Most sake is young, though some connoisseurs prefer the more quirky flavours of an aged version. Budding sake buffs should focus on where it comes from. Sake from Nada, near Kobe, is 'masculine', clean and vigorous in taste; Fushimi, near Kyoto, produces a more delicate, 'feminine' sake. Etiquette demands that, when drinking sake, you fill everyone else's cup but not your own.

SHOCHU

Sake may be the face of Japanese alcohol worldwide, but in its mother country the rice brew is struggling to stay relevant. Young people have turned away from the fragrant brew, with domestic sales on a seemingly irrepressible downward spiral.

Meanwhile, another Japanese drink is surging. Shochu, a drink usually distilled from rice, barley, brown sugar or sweet potatoes, was long seen as the cheap hooch to sake's elegance. But the producers refined their distilling and marketing techniques, and their drink stormed both ends of the market. Convenience stores and *izakaya* (bars that serve food) now do a brisk trade in *chu-hai* drinks (shochu mixed with fruit juice or tea), while specialist bars have popped up to serve high-end shochu with gourmet Japanese food.

The most popular style of shochu is *imo-jochu*, made from sweet potatoes, but it's also the most pungent and arguably least accessible style. A shochu novice might prefer a more neutral *kome-jochu* (rice shochu) or the gentle sweetness of a *kokuto-jochu* (brown sugar shochu). Drink it straight, on the rocks or *mizuwari* (mixed with water).

Okonomiyaki

This is a do-it-yourself pancake or omelette stuffed with seafood and vegetables. You cook it yourself on the table (which has a heated steel surface) and daub it with tasty sauce.

Ramen

Japanese fast food. A bowl of noodles in a meat broth with a variety of toppings. Don't be afraid to slurp while eating.

Robata-yaki

You will find noise, smoke, tasty seafood and vegetables, often charcoal-grilled, hot sake and camaraderie.

Shokudo

Inexpensive, found everywhere and easily recognisable by the displays of plastic food outside, these restaurants normally serve a variety of Western and Japanese food (including the dubious delights of a mixture of the two, such as octopus spaghetti). The cheapest places to eat if you're on a budget.

Soba and udon (noodles)

The Japanese take this cheap and wholesome food very seriously. Noodles are often handmade, rolled and cut in the restaurant; they are served hot, in soup, in winter, or chilled in summer. *Soba* are brown buckwheat noodles, favoured by Tokyo connoisseurs. *Udon* are fat white wheat noodles, popular in Osaka and the south.

Tonkatsu

Deep-fried breaded pork cutlets topped with a special sauce. Normally served as part of a set meal and can almost always be found on a *shokudo*'s menu.

Yakitori (kebabs)

Yakitori is Japanese finger food. Hungry businessmen drop into tiny, smoky stalls, tucked away under the railway arches, where skewerfuls of chicken (including the gizzard, liver and tongue) are grilled over charcoal, other meat and vegetables.

WHERE TO EAT

The Japanese love eating out. There are literally thousands of restaurants, from cheap stand-up noodle shops to some of the world's best and most expensive restaurants. However, Japanese restaurants normally specialise in one type of food, so don't always expect a wide selection to choose from. In this list of recommended restaurants, the star rating indicates the approximate cost per person for a meal, exclusive of alcohol.

★   Up to ¥2,000
★★   ¥2,000–5,000
★★★ ¥5,000–20,000

As a general rule, if there isn't a price list outside it's very expensive.

There is no tipping in Japan. Hotel restaurants will add tax (6 per cent) and service charge (10 per cent).

TOKYO
Japanese cuisine
Akiyoshi ★
Bustling *yakitori*.
Next to Nishi-Ikebukuro Park. Subway: Ikebukuro.
Tel: 03 3982 0644.

Edokko ★
Tempura restaurant.
Next to the shrines.
Subway: Asakusa.
Tel: 03 3841 0150.

Ramen Jiro Mita Honten ★
Cheap, greasy and legendary *ramen*.
2-16-4 Mita, Minato-ku.
Subway: Mita.
No phone.

Shin Hi No Moto ★
(Andy's)
Excellent, friendly *izakaya*.
Near Yurakucho subway station.
Tel: 03 3214 8021.

Tsunahachi ★
Good tempura.
Behind Mitsukoshi department store.
Subway: Shinjuku.
Tel: 03 3358 2788.

Ueno Yabu Soba ★
Famous *soba* restaurant.
Next to Marui department store. Subway: Ueno.
Tel: 03 3831 4728.

Daiwa sushi ★★
After watching Tsukiji's tuna auction, eat fresh sushi for breakfast.
Bldg 6, Tsukiji Market, 5-2-1 Tsukiji, Chuo-ku.
Subway: Tsukiji/Tsukiji-shijo. Tel: 03 3547 6807.

Gaya ★★
Healthy macrobiotic fare.
2-2-5 Shibuya, Shibuya-ku. Subway: Omotesando.
Tel: 03 3498 8810.
www.gaya.co.jp

Hatsuogawa ★★
Venerable eel restaurant.
2-8-4 Kaminarimon, Taito-ku.
Subway: Asakusa.
Tel: 03 3844 2723.

Midori Sushi ★★
Good, well-priced sushi.
1F Ginza 7-108, Korida-dori, Ginza.
Subway: Ginza.
Tel: 03 5568 1212.

Shabuzen ★★
All-you-can-eat *shabu-shabu*, as seen in the film *Lost in Translation*.
Shibuya Creston Hotel, 10-8 Kamiyamacho.
Subway: Shibuya.
Tel: 03 3485 0800.

Soranoniwa ★★
Exquisite soy-based dishes.
4-17 Sakuragaokacho, Shibuya-ku.
JR/subway: Shibuya.
Tel: 03 5728 5191.

Tachimichiya ★★
Punk-rock-themed *izakaya* with great food.
30-8 Sarugakucho, Shibuya-ku.
Subway: Daikanyama.
Tel: 03 5459 3431.

Tokachiya ★★
Hokkaido specialities in a stylish but casual setting.
Ginza Corridor,
6-2 Ginza, Chuo-ku.
JR: Yurakucho/subway:
Ginza. Tel: 03 3573 7373.
www.tokachiya.com

Inakaya ★★★
Famous *robata-yaki* restaurant.
5-3-4 Roppongi.
Subway: Roppongi.
Tel: 03 3408 5040.

Sukiyabashi Jiro ★★★
The sushi restaurant with the best reputation.
4-2-15 Ginza, Chuo-ku.
JR: Yurakucho/subway:
Ginza. Tel: 03 3535 3600.

Tamahide ★★★
Historic chicken hotpot restaurant.
1-17-10 Nihonbashi
Ningyocho, Chuo-ku.
Subway: Ningyocho.
Tel: 03 3668 7651.

International cuisine

Eat More Greens ★
Vegetarian café and bakery.
2-2-5 Azabu-juban.
Subway: Azabu-juban.
Tel: 03 3798 3191.

West Park Café ★
Home-made bread, eggs Benedict and good coffee.

Park Yoyogi-uehara 1F,
23-11 Motoyoyogi-cho.
Subway: Yoyogi-uehara.
Tel: 03 5478 6065.
www.maysfood.com

Asterix ★★
Unpretentious but superb French food.
B1F, 6-3-16 Akasaka.
Subway: Akasaka.
Tel: 03 5561 0980.

Dhaba India ★★
Southern Indian curries.
2-7-9 Yaesu Chuo-ku.
Subway: Kyobashi.
Tel: 03 3272 7160.
www.dhabaindia.com

Fonda de la
Madrugada ★★
Mexican fare in a mock cantina.
2-33-12 Jingumae,
Shibuya-ku.
JR: Harajuku.
Tel: 03 5410 6288.

Mango Tree ★★
Thai food, great views.
Marunouchi Building.
Subway: Tokyo.
Tel: 03 5224 5489.

Shamaim ★★
Israeli buffet.
4-11 Sakaecho, Nerima-ku.
Station: Ekoda.
Tel: 03 3948 5333.

Soushian ★★
Exquisite Korean.
3-24-5 Nishiazabu,
Minato-ku.

Subway: Hiroo/Roppongi.
Tel: 03 3478 2206.

Daini's Table ★★★
Nouvelle Chinese.
6-3-14 Minami Aoyama.
Subway: Omotesando.
Tel: 03 3407 0363.

Mario i Sentieri ★★★
First-rate Italian fare.
4-1-10 Nishi-Azabu,
Minato-ku. Subway:
Hiroo/Roppongi.
Tel: 03 6418 7072.
www.mario-frittoli.com

New York Grill ★★★
Great food, stunning view.
52nd floor Park Hyatt
Tower. Subway: Shinjuku.
Tel: 03 5323 3458.

KAMAKURA

There are plenty of restaurants around the station and towards Hachiman Shrine.

Dengaku ★
Charcoal-grilled tofu and vegetables.
5-minute walk north
of Kamakura station
along Komachi-dori
shopping street.

NIKKO

Local speciality is *yuba* – soft, sweet 'skin' skimmed from soya milk. Look for it in the restaurants around the stations.

KYOTO
Japanese cuisine
Issen Yoshoku ★
Okonomiyaki as fast-food takeaway.
Shijo, Nawate-agaru.
Tel: 075 533 0001.

Yamatomi ★
Great food overlooking the river.
Kawaramachi Shijo-agaru, on Pontocho.
Tel: 075 221 3268.

Gion Matsuno ★★
Specialises in eel.
4th building east of Minami-za Theatre Shijo, Gion. Tel: 075 561 2786.
www.matsuno-co.com

Gogyo ★★
Rich *ramen* in a former geisha's house.
Yanaginobanba, Takoyakushi-sagaru.
Tel: 075 254 5567. www.ramendininggogyo.com

Honke Owariya ★★
Kyoto's oldest *soba* restaurant dates back to the 15th century.
Kurumayacho, Nijo-sagaru. Tel: 075 231 3446.

Minokichi ★★
Venerable and accessible *kaiseki.*
Dobutsuen-mae-dori, Sanjo-agaru, opposite Miyako Hotel.
Tel: 075 771 4185.

Okutan ★★
Tofu in beautiful temple setting; vegetarian.
In Nanzenji.
Tel: 075 771 8709.

Toriyasu ★★
Yakitori for connoisseurs.
Shimbashi-agaru, Nawate-dori, Gion.
Tel: 075 561 7203.

Misoguigawa ★★★
French cuisine meets Kyoto *kaiseki.*
Pontocho Higashigawa, Sanjo-sagaru.
Tel: 075 221 2270.

NARA
Many restaurants are near Kintetsu Nara station.

Yanagi-chaya ★★★
Nara's classiest *kaiseki.*
Just east of Kohfukuji.
Tel: 0742 22 7560.

OSAKA
Go to Dotombori in south Osaka or the malls in Hankyu Grand Building and Shin-Umeda City in the north.

Japanese cuisine
Kinguemon ★
An excellent *ramen* shop.
3-2-8 Fukaekita, Joto-ku.
Tel: 06 6975 8018.

Negiyaki Yamamoto ★
Try *okonomiyaki*, an Osakan speciality, here.
1-8-4 Juso Honmachi, Yodogawa-ku.
Tel: 06 6308 4625. www.negiyaki-yamamoto.com

Gomasuri Chanko ★★
Sumo-style cooking.
2F Griffon Building, 4-7-11 Tenjinbashi.
Station: Ogimachi.
Tel: 06 6357 0120.

Kani Doraku ★★★
Famous crab restaurant.
1-6-18 Dotombori, Chuo-ku.
Tel: 06 6211 8975.

International cuisine
Manryo ★★
Korean barbecue.
1-2-14 Minami Morimachi, Kita-ku.
Tel: 06 6361 1371.

Ponte Vecchio ★★★
Osaka's best Italian food.
1-8-6 Kitahama, Chuo-ku. Tel: 06 6229 7770.

FUKUOKA
There is a good selection of restaurants in the IMS Building, Tenjin, and in Nakasu.

Yoshinaga Unagi ★
World's best eel.
2-8-27 Nakasu.
Tel: 092 271 0700.

Sustainable Japan

At first glance, Japan doesn't seem a particularly eco-friendly country. You will spot that your shopping is excessively, if exquisitely, packaged, and you may notice pricey appliances discarded at roadside collection points, victims of an insatiable appetite for novelty and technology.

But with so many people crowded on to such a small island with so few natural resources, Japan has no choice but to pursue green policies. And as a leader in technology, the country is in a great position to pioneer sustainable living.

In spring 2010, electronics maker Sanyo opened a 'solar car park' for hybrid bicycles in Tokyo's Setagaya ward. For a small fee, locals can borrow one of 40 electric bicycles powered by solar panels and lithium-ion batteries. The scheme is just one of many eco-projects in this innovative, tech-pioneering country.

Also in spring 2010, the Bay Quarter Annex shopping centre opened in Yokohama, just south of Tokyo. Much of the complex's energy is supplied by Japan's largest inbuilt solar panel, covering one wall of the shopping centre.

Elsewhere, cities are collecting and refining used cooking oil to create biofuel for municipal buses. And in Kyoto, the city that gave its name to the famous 1997 Protocol on Climate Change, you can ride eco-taxis with small turbines on the roofs supplying the vehicles' electricity.

Not all of the initiatives are hi-tech, though. Since 2005, the Japanese government has been promoting a 'Cool Biz' campaign to encourage companies to turn the air conditioning down. The policy called for businesses to relax their dress codes and allow employees to work in short-sleeved shirts, without the traditional jacket and tie. And the government-backed *uchimizu* campaign saw ministers spraying water on the streets of Ginza in an effort to persuade people to do likewise outside their homes. The politicians claimed that such behaviour could lower external temperatures by up to a full degree Celsius.

Also in Ginza, some of the high-rise boutique and hotel rooftops are home to unseen eco-projects that seem in stark contrast to the rampant consumerism that characterises the area. Some are covered in greenery, while others have rooftop beehives producing urban honey. Meanwhile, renowned architect Kengo Kuma designed a shopping centre, which opened in Tokyo's Futako Tamagawa district in early 2010, with greenery spilling out over the eaves.

And the good news for some visitors to Japan is that the increasing interest in ecology and sustainability has lead to a boom in vegetarian restaurants and cafés. Though this is still a resolutely meat- and fish-loving country, there are currently around 40 pure vegetarian or vegan restaurants in Tokyo alone, plenty more in Kyoto, and a growing number of places with meat-free meals on their menus.

The traditional Zen cuisine, *shojin ryori*, is pure vegan and still served in temples and some high-end restaurants. Though menus have grown far beyond the humble origins of a priest's sustenance, the Zen principles of sustainable eating practices still hold true and have massively influenced Japanese culture over the centuries.

Visit Japan for Sustainability for more information on other sustainable activities in Japan: www.japanfs.org. Vegetarian restaurant guide: www.vege-navi.jp

Architect Kengo Kuma's eco-friendly shopping centre in a Tokyo suburb features rooftop lawns and mesh pyramids for greenery to cover

Accommodation

The Japanese are inveterate travellers around their own country and Japan is well supplied with hotels; new ones spring up each year. Every major city has towering Western-style hotels, well up to international standards, and plenty of what are called in Japanese 'business hotels', which offer an economical bed for the night. These are usually clustered around the station. A good way to experience genuine Japanese hospitality is to stay in a traditional inn.

Even in Tokyo, hotels are no more expensive than in any Western country and less expensive than in many; in business hotels, a small but immaculately clean room costs between ¥7,500 and ¥10,000. In the countryside a night at a *minshuku* (bed and breakfast) will cost ¥4–8,000.

At luxury hotels, 10 per cent service charge and 6 per cent tax are routinely added to the bill. Outside large Western-style hotels, credit cards are often not accepted. Always take plenty of cash when you travel.

The Japan National Tourism Organization (JNTO) and local TICs provide listings of ryokan and hotels. The JNTO also provides a free booking service if you stay in one of the Japan Welcome Inn group hotels.

Lodging Japanese-style
Ryokan (Inns)

A traditional inn provides a glimpse of the way the Japanese live and is an experience not to be missed.

You slide open the front door, remove your shoes, put on slippers and are escorted to your own *tatami*-matted room. The room will be sparsely furnished, with a futon mattress, which is spread on the floor at bedtime, and quilts to keep you warm in winter or a towelling blanket in summer. There will be a television, a flask of tea and a *yukata* (cotton bathrobe). You bathe before dinner. Be careful to remove slippers before walking on *tatami* and use the special toilet slippers provided; don't forget to soap and rinse yourself outside the bath (*see p21*). Dinner is around 6pm and breakfast at 7–8am.

The price of accommodation always includes two Japanese-style meals. Wear your *yukata* for dinner and expect mountain vegetables and regional specialities.

For a traditional ryokan experience, try **Kansuiro Ryokan** in **Hakone** (*tel: 0460 85 5511; www.kansuiro.co.jp*). A luxurious, modern take is **Hoshinoya** in **Karuizawa, Nagano** (*tel: 0267 45 6000; www.hoshinoya.com*). There are also two legendary ryokan in Kyoto: Tawaraya (*tel: 075 211 5566*) and Hiiragiya (*tel: 075 221 1136; www.hiiragiya.co.jp*).

Local Tourist Information Centres will advise on budget accommodation. The Japan National Tourism Organization publishes a leaflet on the Economical Japanese Inn Group, an association of ryokan geared to foreigners, where English is spoken.

Minshuku
(Bed, breakfast and evening meal)

A *minshuku* is a family home rather like an English or American bed and breakfast. There are *minshuku* all over Japan, even in the tiniest village. You have your own room, but will be expected to lay out your futon yourself (you will find it inside the cupboard). You use a communal bath. Dinner will be Japanese-style, served in a communal room. For the cost of your lodging some offer a veritable feast, while in others the fare is spartan.

Onsen (Spas)

Many Japanese-style inns are in hot-spring resorts. Here the main feature is the vast communal baths, divided into men's and women's, always piping hot and full of health-giving minerals. Sometimes there is a variety of baths – a Jacuzzi®, a whirlpool bath, and baths of different temperatures or different

Japanese luxury in a typical ryokan

mineral contents. The baths are usually in the basement. Most wonderful of all are the *rotemburo*, where the baths are outdoors and you sit under the stars, soaking in steaming water. Dinner will be lavish, often in a huge dining room, with entertainment or karaoke to follow.

Western-style hotels

Japan has a long tradition of Western-style hotels. Some of the oldest – the **Fujiya** in Hakone (1878), the **Kanaya** in Nikko (1873) – are worth visiting in their own right, while Frank Lloyd Wright's **Imperial Hotel**, now partially preserved in Meiji-mura (*see p102*), famously survived the 1923 earthquake.

Business hotels (economical)

Designed for Japanese businessmen on the move, these hotels provide basic, economical and scrupulously clean accommodation. Most rooms are singles, so small that the bed occupies nearly the entire space. There will be a television (often coin-fed), reading lamp and tiny bath and toilet unit moulded out of plastic: all the necessaries (but nothing to encourage you to stay long) at reasonable prices – from ¥7,500 upwards. Ask at the JNTO for the *Business Hotel Guide*.

Capsule hotels

A capsule hotel is like a beehive, with floor upon floor of coffin-sized capsules, each just big enough to hold a bed, television, radio, reading light and alarm clock. Designed for businessmen too late or drunk to get home, most are men-only; a few are women-only.

Love hotels

These are fantasy palaces designed for lovers, whether married or not, in search of privacy from claustrophobic Japanese family life. You can spot them by the outrageous architecture. The weary traveller should note that an overnight stay is not cheap – most people stay only two hours.

Luxury hotels

The luxury chains took a long time to arrive in Japan, but now all the big names are here, including The Peninsula, The Shangri-la, The Conrad, The Mandarin Oriental and a clutch of Hyatts. Though the suites, in all their opulent splendour, cost a small fortune, there are usually well-appointed rooms on the lower floors that offer great value.

Youth hostels

Youth hostels offer a very cheap way to see Japan. Some are not hostels at all, but temples, inns or farms in beautiful locations. There is no age limit. You can often join on the spot, though it is safer to join before you leave home. See *Youth Hostel Handbook*, available from hostels or Japan Youth Hostel Association (*tel: 03 3288 1417*); JNTO publishes *Youth Hostels in Japan*.

Love hotels are anything but discreet, with the large red banner displaying prices for a rest and for an overnight stay

WHERE TO STAY

The following list of suggested hotels will help you select an appropriate place to suit your budget.

★ Under ¥10,000
★★/★★★ ¥10,000–22,000
★★★★ Over ¥22,000

Tokyo

Hotel New Koyo ★
Budget backpacker hostel.
2-26-13 Nihonzutsumi, Taito-ku. Tel: 03 3873 1358. www.newkoyo.jp

Kimi Ryokan ★
Japanese inn for foreigners.
*2-36-8 Ikebukuro, Toshima-ku.
Tel: 03 3971 3766.
www.kimi-ryokan.jp*

Excel Hotel Tokyu ★★★
Inside Shibuya station.
*Shibuya Mark City, 1-12-2 Dogenzaka, Shibuya-ku.
Tel: 03 5457 0109.
www.tokyuhotels.co.jp*

Hotel Villa Fontaine ★★★
A chain of well-appointed, good-value hotels.
www.hvf.jp/eng

Ryokan Shigetsu ★★★
In the heart of nostalgic Asakusa.
1-31-11 Asakusa, Taito-ku.
Tel: 03 3843 2345.
www.shigetsu.com

Park Hyatt Tokyo ★★★★
A truly world-class hotel.
*3-7-1 Nishi-Shinjuku, Shinjuku-ku.
Tel: 03 5322 1234. www. tokyo.park.hyatt.com*

Peninsula Tokyo ★★★★
Great location, stunning design.
*1-8-1 Yurakucho, Chiyoda-ku.
Tel: 03 6270 2888.
www.peninsula.com*

Shangri-La Tokyo ★★★★
The capital's newest luxury hotel.
*Marunouchi Trust Tower, 1-8-3 Marunouchi, Chiyoda-ku.
Tel: 03 6739 7888.
www.shangri-la.com*

Hakone

Laforet Gora ★
Great-value hotel with gorgeous outdoor hot spring.
*1320 Gora, Hakone-machi, Ashigarashimo-gun, Kanagawa.
Tel: 0460 82 2121.*

Gora Tensui ★★★
One of Japan's most luxurious ryokan. Choice of Japanese- or Western-style rooms.
1320-276 Gora,
*Hakone-machi, Ashigarashimo-gun, Kanagawa.
Tel: 0460 86 1411.
www.gora-tensui.com*

Sapporo

Cross Hotel ★★
Stylish, modern and excellent value, close to Sapporo station.
*2-23 Kita-nijo Nishi, Chuo-ku.
Tel: 011 272 0010.
www.crosshotel.com*

JR Tower Nikko Sapporo ★★
Sitting atop JR Sapporo station, it has great views.
*2-5 Kita-gojo Nishi, Chuo-ku.
Tel: 011 251 2222.
www.jrhotelgroup.com/ eng*

Kyoto

K's Guest House ★
Well-appointed, spacious hostel.
*Dotemachi, Shichijo-agaru, Shimogyo-ku.
Tel: 075 342 2444.
www.kshouse.jp*

Nine hours ★
Luxury capsule hotel for men and women.
Teramachi, Shijo-sagaru, Shimogyo-ku.

Tel: 075 353 9005.
www.9hours.jp
Shunkoin ★
Private rooms in a Zen
temple with temple tour
and bicycle hire included.
*42 Myoshinji-cho,
Hanazono, Ukyo-ku.
Tel: 075 462 5488.
www.shunkoin.com*
Ishihara ★★
Great-value ryokan,
favoured by late director
Akira Kurosawa.
*76 Anekoji-agaru, Yanagi-
banba, Nakagyo-ku.
Tel: 075 221 5612.
www.yado-web.com*
Nishiyama Ryokan ★★
Traditional inn geared
to foreign guests.
*Gokomachi, Nijo-sagaru,
Nakagyo-ku.
Tel: 075 222 1166.
www.ryokan-kyoto.com*
Suisenkyo ★★
Private rental of old
townhouse.
*473-15 Umemiya-cho,
Higashiyama-ku.
Tel: 075 712 7023.
www.suisenkyo.com*
Hotel Mume ★★★
Charming boutique hotel
in Gion.
*Shinmonzen, Higashioji
Nishi-iru, Higashiyama-ku.
Tel: 075 525 8787.
www.hotelmume.com*

Hyatt Regency Kyoto ★★★
Kyoto's top western-style
hotel.
*644-2 Sanjusangendo-
mawari, Higashiyama-ku.
Tel: 075 541 1234. www.
kyoto.regency.hyatt.com*
Yoshikawa ★★★
Friendly, family-run
ryokan with famous
tempura restaurant.
*Tominokoji, Oike-sagaru,
Nakagyo-ku.
Tel: 075 221 5544. www.
kyoto-yoshikawa.co.jp*

Osaka
Super Hotel ★
A chain of hotels with
small but excellent-value
rooms.
*Tel: 06 6447 9000.
www.superhotel.co.jp*
**Arietta Hotel &
Osteria** ★★
Cosy, friendly and
convenient. Unbeatable
in this price range.
*3-2-6 Azuchi-machi,
Chuo-ku.
Tel: 06 6267 2787.
www.thehotel.co.jp/en/
arietta_osaka*
**Hotel Villa Fontaine
Shinsaibashi** ★★
Includes ladies' rooms
for solo female travellers.
*3-5-24 Minami-Senba,
Chuo-ku.*

*Tel: 06 6241 1110.
www.hvf.jp/eng*
Dojima Hotel ★★★★
Osaka's hip designer
accommodation.
*2-1-31 Dojimahama, Kita-
ku. Tel: 06 6341 3000.
www.dojima-hotel.com*
**Ritz-Carlton
Osaka** ★★★★
Pure luxury.
*2-5-25 Umeda, Kita-ku.
Tel: 06 6343 7000.
www.ritzcarlton.com*

Fukuoka
Zen Oyado Nishitei ★
Japanese inn in a quiet
neighbourhood.
*1-8-10 Shirogane,
Chuo-ku.
Tel: 092 531 7777. www.
zen-oyado-nishitei.com*
**Hotel Leopalace
Hakata** ★★
Very modern hotel in a
great location.
*2-5-33 Hakataeki-
Higashi, Hakata-ku.
Tel: 092 482 1212.
www.leopalacehotels.jp*
**With the Style
Fukuoka** ★★★★
Stunning, unforgettable
designer hotel.
*1-9-18 Hakataeki-
Minami, Hakata-ku.
Tel: 092 433 3900.
www.withthestyle.com*

The three arts of refinement

The three classical arts of refinement are the tea ceremony (*chado* or *sado*), flower arrangement (*kado* or ikebana) and the lesser-known incense ceremony (*kodo*). Each is a traditional ritual which, despite its simplicity, take years of practice to master.

The tea ceremony first arrived in Japan when Zen monks returned to Japan from China in the 12th century bringing tea with them, which they used as a stimulant to keep themselves awake during hours of meditation. In the 16th century, the tea master Sen no Rikyu laid down the ritual of the Way – the proper way to drink tea.

The tea ceremony involves your host, wearing kimono, serving you powdered green tea using a tiny bamboo scoop, ladled in a little hot water to whisk the tea to a foam. When the bowl is passed to you, bow, take it and turn it clockwise so that the front is away from you. Sip the tea, wipe the bowl where you drank with your fingers and turn it anticlockwise. There are tearooms in many temples, palaces and castles. One of the oldest is Nanzenji in Kyoto (*see pp88–9*).

Similarly, *kodo* involves taking turns to carefully prepare censers of incense, turning each censer anti-clockwise three times and breathing

Items for the incense ceremony

A typical ikebana arrangement

in the different fragrance of each, before passing it on. The experience of appreciating incense is a beautifully calming and meditative one.

There are vast numbers of ikebana schools around Japan where you can learn the art of flower arrangement. Ikebana originated with the Buddhist ritual of offering flowers to the dead and has since become entwined with Japanese tradition. Each arrangement is asymmetrical rather than the traditional flower arrangements of the West. To find out where to learn ikebana, try Ikebana International (*www.ikebanahq.or*).

There are very few places to experience the incense ceremony. For a long time it was only available to the very wealthy as incense had to be imported from India and China. These days, the best option is Yamada Matsu Koboku, a 200-year-old incense specialist, which offers informal incense sessions above its Kyoto shop. *Muromachi-dori, Shimodachiuri-agaru, Kamigyo-ku, Kyoto. Tel: 075 441 4694.*

Practical guide

Arriving and departing

Entry formalities

Tourists from most European countries and the USA are granted an automatic entry permit for visits of up to 90 days.

By air

There are direct flights to Japan from most major destinations. The national carrier is Japan Airlines. A popular choice is Virgin Atlantic (to and from Narita).

Most visitors arrive at **Narita**, recently expanded, but inconveniently far from Tokyo. If your main destination is Osaka or Kyoto, you can fly straight to **Kansai International Airport**, the futuristic 24-hour airport in Osaka Bay.

To and from Narita: The **limousine bus** linking the airport with TCAT (Tokyo City Air Terminal) and selected hotels is best for those with heavy luggage. Buy tickets from the Airport Limousine Bus Information Desk in the arrivals lobby. Allow up to two hours for the journey. From TCAT take a taxi to your hotel. On departure, check in your baggage at TCAT and take the limousine bus to the airport. **Taxi** from Narita to Tokyo is prohibitively expensive.

You can also get into town by **train**. The Keisei Skyliner train departs from Narita about every 30 minutes and takes one hour to reach Ueno station in northeast Tokyo. You can also catch a regular train to Ueno station (Keisei Line), which is cheaper (but no seat reservations if you have a lot of luggage). It takes about 1½ hours.

The Narita Express (N'EX) train connects Narita Airport with Tokyo, Shinjuku and Yokohama stations. It takes around an hour to reach Tokyo station. In late 2009, new models of N'EX trains were unveiled, with features including power sockets in every chair and lockable luggage holds. The Narita Express is slightly more expensive (though you can use your JR Pass – *see p22*) and takes one hour to Tokyo station. But beware! While seats are usually available going into Tokyo, the Express is often booked up days in advance for the journey out to Narita.

To and from Kansai International Airport: Hi-tech **trains** link the airport with the mainland. The Rapit takes 29 minutes to Namba, Osaka's southern terminus. JR's Haruka reaches Shin-Osaka (for the bullet train line and northern Osaka) in 45 minutes, Kyoto in 75 minutes. Trains depart every 30 minutes. There are **limousine buses** to Osaka, Kobe and Nara; you can also take a **ferry** to Osaka and Kobe. On departure, JAL passengers can check in at City Air Terminals in Namba Nankai and Kyoto stations.

Practical guide

WEATHER CONVERSION CHART

25.4mm = 1 inch

$°F = 1.8 \times °C + 32$

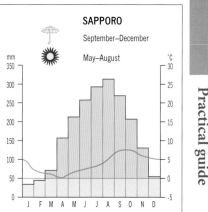

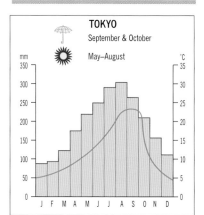

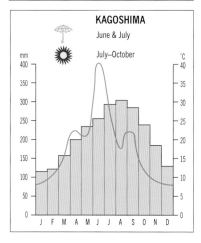

Climate

Spring (March until early May) is warm and dry. June is wet and sultry, and mid-July to late August is hot and humid. Autumn is mild and dry, though September brings occasional typhoons. In winter in the north and on the Sea of Japan coast there is deep snow.

Clothing

Take clothes that will enable you to sit comfortably and decorously on the floor when required, and comfortable walking shoes which can be easily slipped on and off. In spring and autumn you will need a sweater, in summer the lightest of clothing, in winter an overcoat.

In Japan appearance is very important. Most Japanese wear smart, new clothes; you will feel out of place in old or torn clothes. Although there are plenty of shops selling shoes and clothes, it can be difficult to find items in large sizes. Clothes for people over

Camping

Camping has begun to boom in Japan. Travellers with tents are welcome in campsites in national parks in Hokkaido, Tohoku and Kyushu. Campsites also often provide bungalow accommodation.

CONVERSION TABLE

FROM	TO	MULTIPLY BY
Inches	Centimetres	2.54
Feet	Metres	0.3048
Yards	Metres	0.9144
Miles	Kilometres	1.6090
Acres	Hectares	0.4047
Gallons	Litres	4.5460
Ounces	Grams	28.35
Pounds	Grams	453.6
Pounds	Kilograms	0.4536
Tons	Tonnes	1.0160

To convert back, divide by the number in the third column.

MEN'S SHOES

Japan	26	26.5	27.5	28	29	29.5
UK		7	7.5	8.5	9.5	10.5	11
Rest of Europe	41	42	43	44	45	46
USA		8	8.5	9.5	10.5	11.5	12

WOMEN'S SHOES

Japan	24	24.5	25	25.5	25.5	26
UK		4.5	5	5.5	6	6.5	7
Rest of Europe	38	38	39	39	40	41
USA		6	6.5	7	7.5	8	8.5

1.8m (6ft) tall are sold in some major department stores.

Measurements and sizes

Japan uses the metric system. There are various sizing systems, depending on the origin of the item; the terms S, M, L, XL are also understood and used.

Crime

Japan has a famously low crime rate. You can leave your bag unattended and it will be there when you get back. There is plenty of organised crime, run by the notorious *yakuza* crime syndicates, but this does not affect tourists.

Customs regulations

Individual travellers may import duty free: 400 cigarettes, 100 cigars or 500g tobacco; three 760cc bottles of alcoholic drinks; 57ml perfume; and souvenirs to a total value of ¥200,000. It is extremely unwise to take illegal drugs into or out of Japan; if you are carrying prescription medicines take a letter from your doctor.

Driving

See pp22–3.

Electricity

The standard electric current is 100 volts, at 50 cycles in eastern Japan and 60 cycles in the west of the country. Europeans will need an adaptor.

Embassies and consulates

All embassies are in Tokyo. For countries other than those listed below, check the *Yellow Pages* directory.
Australia *2-1-14 Mita, Minato-ku. Tel: 03 5232 4111. www.australia.or.jp*
Canada *7-3-38 Akasaka, Minato-ku. Tel: 03 5412 6200. www.canadanet.or.jp*
Ireland *8-7 Kojimachi, Chiyoda-ku. Tel: 03 3263 0695. www.embassy-avenue.jp/ireland*
New Zealand *20-40 Kamiyama-cho, Shibuya-ku. Tel: 03 3467 2271. www.nzembassy.com/japan*
UK *1 Ichiban-cho, Chiyoda-ku. Tel: 03 5211 1100. www.ukinjapan.fco.gov.uk/en*

USA *1-10-5 Akasaka, Minato-ku.*
Tel: 03 3224 5000.
http://tokyo.usembassy.gov

Emergency telephone numbers
Police *110*
Ambulance/Fire *119*
Tokyo English Life Line (Japanese
Samaritans) *Tel: 03 5774 0992.*
www.telljp.com

Health
There is no need to worry about health.
Food hygiene is better than in most
Western countries. Avoid raw fish in the
hottest summer months.

Be sure to take out travel insurance
to cover health: Japan has all the
medical facilities one would expect,
but both doctors and dentists are
expensive.

Major hotels have lists of English-
speaking staff and some have medical
clinics. Or call **Tokyo Metropolitan
Health and Medical Information Center**
(*tel: 03 5285 8181*; English-speaking
staff) to find your nearest doctor. As a
last resort, call your embassy.

Insurance
Make sure that you are adequately
covered for medical expenses or
repatriation in the case of accident or
illness. A good policy should also include
third party liability, legal assistance, loss
of personal possessions (including cash,
traveller's cheques and documents) and
should have some facility for cancellation
and delay in travel arrangements. Travel

insurance policies can be purchased
through branches of Thomas Cook and
most travel agents.

Language
See pp186–7.

Lost property
Most Japanese are scrupulous about
handing in lost property. If it is not
where you left it, try the nearest police
box. Public transport and taxis have a
lost and found service. Or ring:
**Tokyo Central Metropolitan Police
Board**, Lost and Found office,
tel: 03 3501 0110.
www.keishicho.metro.tokyo.jp
In Osaka:
JR Lost & Found, *tel: 06 6346 4406.*

Maps
The best maps are free and issued by
the JNTO (Japan National Tourism
Organization). For more detail, get
the Kodansha Bilingual Atlases of
Tokyo and Japan. The Japanese-
language Mapple maps are the best
for driving.

Media
There is a wide range of English-
language media, including four
national dailies. Non-English-speaking
foreigners are less well served. In major
cities, foreign-language newspapers
and magazines are available from
specialist bookshops. Many television
programmes are bilingual if you have
the correct receiver.

Money matters

Most people carry wads of cash, which reflects the low crime rate. The currency is the yen, in denominations of 1, 5, 10, 50, 100 and 500 yen coins, and 1,000, 2,000, 5,000 and 10,000 yen notes. Buy yen before you leave home; the exchange rate is usually better than in Japan.

In the major cities, credit cards can be used. Most ATMs are found inside banks and are closed from the early evening. Shinsei and Citibank branches stay open 24 hours, though only Citibank will let you withdraw cash on a foreign credit card. Post offices also have ATMs that accept foreign credit cards, though most close at night.

National holidays

1 January New Year's Day
Second Monday in January Coming of Age Day
11 February National Foundation Day
20 March Spring Equinox
29 April Green Day
3 May Constitution Day
4 May Greenery Day
5 May Children's Day
Third Monday in July Maritime Day
Third Monday in September Respect for the Aged Day
23 September Autumn Equinox
Second Monday in October Health-Sports Day
3 November Culture Day
23 November Labour Thanksgiving Day
23 December Emperor's Birthday.
Banks and public offices close on national holidays. Museums,

restaurants, shops and department stores only close on New Year's Day. The week starting 1 January is an unofficial holiday, as is Golden Week, 29 April–5 May.

Opening hours

Bank opening times vary depending on size. Most open at 9am and close at 3–6pm. ATMs are very rarely 24 hour and most stop working by 10pm. Most department stores open 10am–7pm and close one day a week (the day differs for each). Other shops generally open daily 10am–8pm; most neighbourhoods have a 24-hour supermarket. For post offices *see opposite*. Most museums close on Mondays.

Organised tours

There are many companies offering regular package tours to major cities and regions. Ask the Japan National Tourism Organization (JNTO) for details.

Pharmacies

Japanese pharmacies are well stocked, with many American and European medicines, vitamins and cosmetics.
The American Pharmacy (*tel: 03 5220 7716*) is easily the best and most convenient. Pharmacies in major hotels specialise in imported Western items. There are no 24-hour pharmacies. Hospitals also supply drugs.

Photography

The latest cameras don't appear any earlier in Japan than elsewhere, but you might find a bargain in one of the major electronics retailers in Shinjuku, Shibuya or Akihabara. Memory cards are widely available, but film is hard to come by so stock up before you leave.

Places of worship

There are Shinto shrines and Buddhist temples everywhere. There is also a sizeable Christian population and churches of many denominations in every major city. The following churches in Tokyo hold services in English:
Anglican St Alban's, *3-6-25 Shiba-koen, Minato-ku. Tel: 03 3431 8534. www.saintalbans.jp*
Baptist Tokyo Baptist Church, *9-2 Hachiyama-cho, Shibuya-ku. Tel: 03 3461 8425. www.tokyobaptist.org*
Catholic St Ignatius, *6-5 Kojimachi, Chiyoda-ku. Tel: 03 3263 4584.*

There is also a **synagogue** – Jewish Community of Japan, *3-8-8 Hiroo, Shibuya-ku (tel: 03 3400 2559, www.jcjapan.or.jp)*. Hindus and Muslims are not as well provided for.

Police

Japan is a safe and peaceful country partly because it is so well policed. There are police boxes (*koban*) on practically every corner. The police are courteous and friendly, and though their English may be limited they will draw you a map to show you your way. However, if you get on the wrong side of the law you will see another side of the police. If the offence is serious, contact your embassy.

Post offices

Most post offices are open 9am–5pm Monday to Friday, 9am–noon Saturday. Main post offices are open 9am–7pm Monday to Friday, 9am–3pm Saturday. The stamp counter of the Central Post Office opposite Tokyo station is open 24 hours. Post offices and postboxes are marked by a large red T with two horizontal bars. Use a central post office for international parcels.

Public transport

See pp23–4.

Senior citizens

Discounts of 25 per cent are available on JAL, ANA and JAS airlines for over-65s; proof of age, for example, a passport, is required on purchase. For railway travel the JR Pass, purchasable only outside Japan, is far better value than the discount available for over-65s.

Student and youth travel

Discounts of 35 per cent on internal flights are available on JAL, ANA and JAS airlines for under-21s (SKYMATE scheme). To register for the scheme, bring a passport, 3cm (1¼-inch) square photo and ¥1,000 registration fee to a major airline office. Japan has an excellent youth hostel network (*see p174*).

Sustainable tourism

Thomas Cook is a strong advocate of ethical and fairly traded tourism and
(*Cont. on p188*)

Language

While written Japanese is enormously complicated to read and write, basic spoken Japanese is surprisingly simple. It is not difficult to pick up a few phrases that will make your travels easier.

Pronunciation is straightforward, similar to Spanish or Italian. Pronounce each word phonetically, exactly as it is written, and you will be understood. There is no tone system as in Chinese. Give each syllable equal stress. Intonation is fairly flat.

Note that 'ii' is pronounced as the 'ee' in feet.

Titles Always use surname, not first name, plus -san after the name as the equivalent of Mr, Mrs or Ms (never use any title for yourself). Children are -chan. In formal situations you might be addressed as -sama.

Imported words You will be surprised at how many words come from Western languages. Often you can simply use an English word with Japanese pronunciation and be understood.

BASIC PHRASES

Good morning	ohayo gozaimasu	**Sorry, excuse me**	sumimasen
Good afternoon	konnichi-wa	**Sorry**	gomen nasai
Good evening	konban-wa	**Excuse me**	sumimasen
Good night	oyasumi-nasai	(to call waiter, shop staff, etc)	
How are you?	o-genki-desu-ka?	**Excuse me, do you**	sumimasen, Eigo
Yes, please	o-negai-shimasu	**speak English?**	hanashimasu-ka?
No, thank you	ii-desu	**I don't understand**	wakarimasen
Please	dozo	**Please take me to**	made onegai shimasu
(help yourself, go ahead)		**How much will it**	made ikura desu ka . . . ?
Please give me	o kudasai	**cost to go to . . . ?**	
Yes, just a little	hai, sukoshi dake	**It's an emergency**	kinkyu jitai desu
No, I can't/that's	ie, dame desu	**I'm lost**	michi ni mahoi mashita
not allowed		**Today**	kyo
Thanks	domo	**Tomorrow**	ashita
Thank you	domo arigato	**Yesterday**	kino
Thank you very	domo arigato	**Tonight**	kon'ya
much	gozaimash'ta		
Goodbye	ja mata		
(see you again)			
Goodbye	sayonara		
(farewell)			

NUMBERS

1	ichi	7	nana/shichi
2	ni	8	hachi
3	san	9	kyu/ku
4	yon/shi	10	ju
5	go	100	hyaku
6	roku	1,000	sen

These are combined to make larger numbers, e.g. 18 (ju hachi), 23 (ni ju san), 241 (ni hyaku yon ju ichi)

EMERGENCIES

Help!	tasukete!
Watch out!	abunai!
It hurts!	itai!
I feel ill	kibun ga yokunai

DIRECTIONS

Straight ahead	masugu
Right	migi
Left	hidari
Stop here	koko ni tomatte kudasai
I want to go to	e ikitai no desu ga

IMPORTED WORDS

coffee	kohi
bread	pan
beer	biru
cigarettes	tabako
television	terebi
hotel	hoteru
building	biru
apartment	apato
platform [for trains]	homu ('form')
free gift	sabisu ('service')
bargain breakfast	mawning savisu
	('morning service')
England	Igirisu
France	Furansu

COUNTERS

When listing objects, animals or people, a 'counter' must follow the cardinal number. There are a large number of these counter words, the most useful being:

people	nin
time	ji
floor of a building	kai
2 o'clock	ni ji
8th floor	hachi kai

When asking how many of something, 'nan' is placed before the counter, e.g. nan nin desu ka? (how many people?)

DINING

Menu, please	menu o kudasai
Just a little, please	sukoshi
That's enough	mo ii desu
	itadakimasu
(before starting a meal)	
Thank you,	gochiso sama
that was good	desh'ta
(on finishing a meal)	
This is good	oishi desu
(of food)	
That was good	oishikatta desu
(of food)	
Water, please	mizu kudasai
Knife and fork,	naifu to hawk,
please	kudasai
Chopsticks are fine	hashi de ii desu

QUESTIONS

What is your name?	o namae wa?
My name is Smith	watashi wa Smith desu
How much is it?	ikura desu ka?
Where is the (toilet/hotel/station)?	(toilay/hotel/eki) wa doko desu ka?
Does this train/ bus go to . . . ?	kono kisha/basu wa . . . e ikimasu-ka?
What station is this?	koko wa nani-eki desu ka?
What's the next station?	tsugi wa nani-eki desu ka?

believes that the travel experience should be as good for the places visited as it is for the people who visit them. That's why we firmly support The Travel Foundation, a charity that develops solutions to help improve and protect holiday destinations, their environment, traditions and culture. To find out what you can do to make a positive difference to the places you travel to and the people who live there, please visit *www.thetravelfoundation.org.uk*

Telephones

Japan has a very efficient telephone system. Please note that toll-free numbers beginning *0120* can't be dialled from mobile phones.

Public telephones

Public telephones are colour coded: pink, red and blue are for local calls, which cost ¥10 per minute. Lift the receiver, insert ¥10 and dial. Yellow and green take ¥100 and are useful for long-distance domestic calls.

A low-carbon street light

International calls

Grey telephones and green telephones with a special sign, marked in English and Japanese, are for international calls. Outside Tokyo, it is often difficult to direct dial an international call from your hotel room. It is much cheaper to use a green telephone. To make an international call, *dial 001* to route the call through KDDI, the official international telecom company. If you are using a home or office telephone, there are other companies which offer cheaper rates: ITJ (*dial 0041*) and IDC (*dial 0061*). Public telephones, however, are operated by KDDI, so *dial 001*.

Telephone cards are on sale everywhere. Or you can use most national charge cards and call direct. To call the operator in your home country direct in order to make a collect call or a call via a charge card, *dial 0039* + country code + *1*.

For example, UK operator: *0039 441*; US operator: *0039 11*.

Using your mobile

If you have a 3G handset, your mobile phone should work in Japan. Otherwise you can rent a handset at international airports. Try JAL ABC Rental Phone (*tel: 03 3545 1003; www.jalabc.com*).

Useful numbers

English Directory Enquiries *03 3277 1010*.

Internal collect calls *106*.

To make a domestic long-distance call and check the charge *100*.

Internet

Visit the local Tourist Information
Centre for information on the location
of internet cafés, or try Kinko's (*tel:
0120 001 966*), which offers computers
with internet service.

Time

Japan is 9 hours ahead of Greenwich
Mean Time. There is no daylight saving,
so the difference is 8 hours in summer.

Tipping

There is no tipping in Japan – in fact, it
might even be considered an insult. All
hotels and some restaurants will
automatically add 10 per cent service
charge to your bill.

Toilets

A Japanese word for toilet is *toi-lay*.
There are toilets in hotels, restaurants,
department stores and stations, and
these are usually clearly indicated by a
symbol of a man or a woman. They
may be Western-style or designed for
squatting, Japanese-style. Knock on a
closed door; an answering knock means
that it is occupied. Always carry a
supply of tissues.

Tourist offices

Japan National Tourism Organization
(JNTO) offices have knowledgeable
staff, who usually speak several
languages and issue excellent maps,
leaflets and information on current
cultural events. They will help you with
travel plans and hotel reservations.

JNTO abroad

Australia *Level 18, Australia Square
Tower, 264 George Street, Sydney,
NSW 2000. Tel: 02 9251 3024.*
UK *Heathcoat House, 20 Savile Row,
London W15 3PR. Tel: 020 7734 9638.*
USA *One Rockefeller Plaza, Suite 1250,
New York, NY 10020. Tel: 212 757 5640.*

In Japan

In Japan, the JNTO operates Tourist
Information Centres (TICs) in Tokyo
and Kyoto, and at Narita and Kansai
International Airports. Offices are open
9am–5pm, Monday to Friday.
TIC Tokyo Office *IF Metropolitan
Government Building No 1, 2-8-1 Nishi-
Shinjuku, Shinjuku-ku. Tel: 03 5321 3077.*
Japan Travel Phone, operated by JNTO,
provides information and assistance in
English, wherever you are, 9am–5pm,
Monday to Friday (*tel: 03 3201 3331*).

There are two other telephone
information services: **Information
Corner**, *tel: 045 671 7209* and **Japan
Helpline**, *tel: 0120 461 997*.

Travellers with disabilities

Many public facilities, including toilets,
are equipped to cater for people with
disabilities and wheelchairs are
provided at many major sights. Most
hotels are equipped to cope with
wheelchairs, but railway stations are a
nightmare. With advance notice help
can be provided at Narita Airport.

Contact the Japanese Red Cross for
information (*tel: 03 3438 1311;
www.jrc.or.jp*).

Index